AM I A CHAP?

AM I A CHAP?

SUBMIT YOURSELF TO
THE ULTIMATE SARTORIAL
INSPECTION

GUSTAV TEMPLE

Beautiful
Books

First published 2011.

Beautiful Books Limited
36-38 Glasshouse Street
London W1B 5DL

www.beautiful-books.co.uk

ISBN 9781905636815

9 8 7 6 5 4 3 2 1

Cover design by Ian Pickard.
Book design by Hugh Adams, AB3 Design.
Printed and bound in the UK by Butler, Tanner & Dennis.

PHOTO CREDITS
Cover photo: Russ Bell
Author photo: Elisabeth Blanchet
Mary Evans Picture Library: Pages 29, 45, 47, 63, 79, 129, 131, 165, 167,185
Russ Bell: Pages 21, 39, 73, 87, 145, 159, 179.
Fiona Campbell: Pages 57, 93, 105.
Barima Nyantekyi: Page 123
Getty Images: Page 149

To Theodore and Romilly, my favourite Chap and Chapette.
And to M.

Contents

1. THE COUNTRY

"It is my belief, Watson, founded upon my experience, that the lowest and vilest alleys of London do not present a more dreadful record of sin than does the smiling and beautiful countryside."
SHERLOCK HOLMES

The Country Squire

On the verge of extinction, the Country Squire doggedly holds on to his tenuous position in the local village (which his grandfather owned). Where once his tweedy form was greeted with much tugging of forelocks, he now rarely makes it to the village shop without being mugged. He still enjoys his Sunday pint in the Lamb & Flag, but it is consumed against the deafening roar of televised association football and he must share his table with second homers studiously reading the Farrow & Ball colour chart.

HABITAT

What's left of his estate, now that a retail park has been built next door and driven most of the wildlife away.

FEEDING

The lady who "does" for him has been trained never to cook anything that doesn't appear in Elizabeth David's seminal tome from the 1950s. She once tried to enter the house clutching a book by Jamie Oliver, but it was confiscated before she could reach the kitchen.

MATING

A disastrous early marriage left our Squire licking his wounds for decades, and the closest he gets to carnal pleasure these days is when his three Labradors jump on to his bed.

MIGRATION

The Squire has no need for holidays, because every Summer members of his ex-wife's family descend on the house and pretend he isn't there, while drinking their way through his drinks cabinet and wrecking his billiard table.

Country Chaps

Lord Wonston's photograph came with this breezy missive: "Well, there ain't a mustache in sight, but me togs ain't too far off .... in mufti, from the Reg'ment dontcha know!"
Someone seems to have locked him in a broom cupboard, and that is the best place for him.

"This is me in Suffolk in my best tweed suit with appropriate twill shirt, wool tie, green braces, brown shoes and socks. Am I chap?" asks Sean Rillo Raczka.
No, you are just a very boring man in a field. With a particularly unimaginative pair of spectacles. You look as though you could do with a girlfriend. Or simply a friend.

This is a perfect example of how true Chappism is not always taking the obvious route. Of these three sprightly coves out for a country stroll, only one has mastered his wardrobe adequately to the task.

The fellow on the right has no idea what coat size he takes; the middle man is too dull to contemplate. The chap on the left, however, has dressed practically for a rugged walk, yet with enough sartorial flourishes to make him a pleasant sight to other walkers.

Quick, call the gamekeeper! One of the salmon has escaped the loch and dressed itself as a student. Will these fish stop at nothing to squeeze yet more subsidies out of the government?

Country Chaps

Sven Shaw, of Ropley, has broken in his tweeds sufficiently before airing them in public. We cannot see what he is wearing under his coat, but his boutonnière would suggest that he is wearing the correct corduroys or moleskins. He has also incorporated the bunting as part of his outfit, which shows imagination and panache.

"I have been wearing cravats for years," writes John Biles, "and wondering why no one else was." Because they didn't want to look anything like you or be connected with you in any way whatsoever. As soon as you cease wearing cravats, we can all go back to enjoying them again. Even the corrugated iron church is more stylish than you.

They are running out of ideas in the horror movie genre. Having made films about killer rats, sharks, monkeys, snakes and robots, they have now decided to unleash this terrifying group of zombie chaps on the cinema-going public.

Their amazing powers of destruction and viciousness are legion; but what will kill you first of all is their appalling raiment.

D. C. McGregor-Harper sought to amuse with this missive: "Have you seen my bloody dog madam?" I enquired. "What's it look like?" she replied. "You know, brown and white 'bout this big, pheasant in mouth. That reminds me, where'd I put my gun!"

This is what happens when rural families keep inbreeding until there is not a sensible gene left in the entire family. Nor even a sensible waistcoat.

Groups of Chaps

"**A**re we chap?" asked this group, under the aegis of Kate Sibley.

Frankly, no. You are nothing more than a group of thoroughly ordinary people wearing false moustaches. Some of you haven't even bothered to get changed out of your PE kit, and none of you have made so much as a cursory glance into the vintage clothing emporium behind you for some decent clothes. Get back to university and try and learn something useful.

At least three of these men are wearing jeans; two of them are sporting plimsolls; not one of them has genuine facial hair; and one is clearly a homosexual. The fact that they are only pretending to be drunk throws a question mark over their nationality, for if they were true Englishmen at least one of them would have fallen into the water by now.

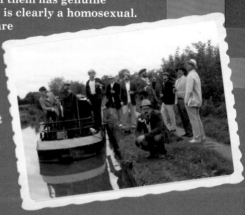

"One of our fund-raising days for the drama department of our college," writes Harrison Lee, "involved my friend Sebastian and I dressing in 1930s hunting attire while another associate dressed as 'The Bear' was chased about the complex."

Was it not an innocent caper such as this that resulted in the Columbine massacre? Put your weapons down, fellows, and replace them with briars, meerschaums and churchwardens.

Groups of Chaps

In group photographs such as this, there is usually something to cling to. A nicely turned cuff, a well-knotted tie, or even just a winsome smile, which reveals one of their number to be at least heading in the vague direction of Chappishness.

If your average non-chap saw this lot in a pub, they would probably instinctively think "What a bunch of w***kers."

For once, the Chap is inclined to agree.

"At a stag do held at a country manor," writes Alex Crawley, "the stag had spent the last 4 years in the US and required urgent re-anglicisation. He is in the centre in the red frock coat."

And the rest of you are comfortable in your Englishness? Well, you shouldn't be. Re-Anglicisation is too good for you – the only suitable recourse would be immediate repatriation to whichever godforsaken island of doom you crawled ashore from. Or was it Australia?

We've heard all the rumours about randy vicars and here's the proof: this old rogue seems to have sired an entire congregation – and the only one who has a clue how to dress like a gentleman happens to be a lady!

Andrew Fletcher

Mr. Fletcher dresses people for the moving pictures. When directors of films such as Atonement, Vera Drake and Saving Private Ryan want their cast to be costumed as authentically as possible for a particular period, the Bakelite telephone rings in Andrew's 1930s house in north west London, and if he isn't too busy lengthening the sleeves on a 1940s Harris tweed sports jacket that the original tailor didn't have the decency to make exactly in his size, he pads across the original parquet floor to take the call.

Mr. Fletcher is fortunate to have found a career that reflects his passion for the 1930s and 1940s. His house has been so lovingly fitted with period detail that the 21st century barely gets its foot in the door. Everything, from the curtains to the cooker to the fridge to the lawn mower, is an authentic item from the period he adores.

Mr. Fletcher started collecting Second World War uniforms as a child, progressing to civilian clothing in his teens, and now has a plethora of outfits for every eventuality – even for the beach, where he may be found resplendent in a pair of knitted 1940s swimming trunks. He sees no point in buying even modern undergarments: aside from the fact that they are not particularly comfortable, there is more than enough "dead stock" (ie unused and unsold) vintage underwear around for his needs.

The question could be asked: if he finds contemporary clothing so abhorrent, does he want everyone to dress as he does? Practically speaking, no, but in a sense he is dressing up large swathes of the population – they just happen to be extras in the films he works on.

"I'D RATHER HAVE A 1940S HOOVER THAT LOOKS GOOD AND STILL WORKS AFTER 70 YEARS, THAN AN UGLY ONE THAT WILL PROBABLY BREAK AFTER FIVE MINUTES AND HAVE TO BE THROWN AWAY"

The Hacking Jacket

A hacking jacket is a tweed jacket whose original purpose was to be worn while hacking, or riding in non-formal occasions. Just as the blazer contains vestiges of its naval origins and the morning coat of its hunting origins, so does the hacking jacket, today worn at informal country occasions and in town (though preferably not after six pm). Some cheeky little upstarts even wear a hacking jacket with jeans, but they are probably out to cause trouble and can be disregarded entirely. It should be worn with moleskin or corduroy trousers, which can be of any colour except black or white.

The hacking jacket's equestrian origins can be seen in some of its features. A hacking jacket always has a central rear vent, rather than a pair of side vents. This was to allow the skirt to spread around the saddle with elegance. The pockets are slanted, preventing one's hip flask, cigarette case or copy of *The Chap* to fly out while one's nag jumps over a ditch. Many hacking jackets also feature a tab and button on either lapel, sometimes concealed, which allows the lapels to be buttoned up over one's throat in severe weather.

The fact that the tab is now often added as a feature but never used is indicative of the hacking jacket's evolution from country seat to a seat on the number 38 bus to Clapton. Americans prefer to call a hacking jacket a sports jacket, for no apparent reason other than to annoy us. Ladies can wear hacking jackets; in fact they flatter the female form very well with their classically pinched waists and wide skirts.

There is much argument within tailoring circles regarding the third little pocket

—※—

AMERICANS PREFER TO CALL A HACKING JACKET A SPORTS JACKET, FOR NO REASON OTHER THAN TO ANNOY US

—※—

commonly seen on hacking jackets, above the right-hand front pocket. This has no equestrian purpose and has probably been added since the jacket faded into urban or non-riding use. It is primarily a ticket pocket, and a gentleman out hacking in the 19th century would have had no use for bus, railway or tickets of any other kind.

The Brogue

The word Brogue comes from *bróg*, the Scottish word for shoe, and *bróig*, its Irish equivalent. The origins of the style itself are claimed by both Scots and Irish, whose farm workers would punch holes in their shoes to let out the water from the bogs which had seeped in. Given the weather conditions in both countries, they are probably both accurate.

The holes were punched only through the outer layer on the toe cap, where the leather had double layers. This allows for quick drying without compromising the weather resistance of the uppers. These traditional farmers' shoes first made their way into fashion when the intricate swirling patterns, removed from their practical use, began appearing on ladies' shoes as decoration. Soon the patterns were all over men's shoes too. Initially the brogue was the formal shoe worn with a kilt in Scotland, and always black.

Its transition back to the original brown and back to the country did not happen until the Edwardian era.

Having been "discovered" recently by big fashion houses, today you can find a pair of brogues in purple snakeskin with stiletto heels, should such a thing be of any interest other than anthropological. A pair of men's brogues are preferable in brown (black brogues are a pointless affectation and merely confuse the lines between town and country. Black Oxfords in town, please), and are always better with open lacing. Closed lacing (where the lace section of the shoe goes under the front section) suits more formal shoes like Oxfords, though can be successful on half brogues.

—⁂—

INITIALLY THE BROGUE WAS THE FORMAL SHOE WORN WITH A KILT IN SCOTLAND, AND ALWAYS BLACK

—⁂—

The secret to obtaining a complex and mysterious patina on brown shoes is to alternate between mid-tan and light tan polish. The resulting effect is not unlike that found on Chinese lacquering, with the sense of a faint imprint behind the upper layer of colour. The patina of a brogue polished in this manner will actually improve with age, as long as the shoes are regularly resoled by the maker, which will stretch the leather over the original last.

Ian Carmichael

Ian Carmichael played the upper class twit in a series of films and television programmes in the 1960s, providing a bumbling but well-meaning counterpoint to the cads and bounders who shared the screen with him. He played Bertie Wooster in the 1960s BBC series Jeeves and Wooster, with Dennis Price as Jeeves. Although in his late 40s when he took the role of PG Wodehouse's well-meaning oaf (supposedly fresh out of university), Carmichael captured the spirit of Bertie in a way few actors have managed.

Carmichael was particularly proud of his portrayal of Dorothy L Sayers's aristocratic detective in the television series Lord Peter Wimsey (1972-1975), envying him his aristocratic insouciance, style and intellect. Carmichael's tour-de-force was in School for Scoundrels, in which he played the downtrodden office worker who enrolls at the eponymous Academy to learn the art of One-upmanship, eventually triumphing over the caddish Raymond Delaunay (Terry-Thomas) to win the love of April (Janette Scott).

While Ian Carmichael was no dandy, he dressed with impeccable Englishness at all times, and his lifestyle was that of a quintessential Chap. His war service in the Royal Armoured Corps included landing on the Normandy beaches on D-Day Plus Three and campaigning through France and into Germany. When clambering from the turret of a Valentine tank, he accidentally slammed the lid down on his left hand, depriving him of the top joint of his middle finger. "Dashed unfortunate," was how he viewed the incident. Nevertheless, he was demobilised in 1947 with the rank of major and mentioned in dispatches.

Carmichael's popularity was long-lived because of his universal appeal, both to women – who wanted to mother him – and to men, who sympathised with his blundering reactions to life's difficulties and did not see him as a threat to their wives or girlfriends. So he was neither a true gentleman nor a cad, but something in between. Ian Carmichael captured the spirit of the age and made it alright to be slightly ineffectual, as long as one was immaculately turned out and able to wear a monocle with conviction.

Edward VII

It has been a long tradition in this country to breed excellently dressed Princes of Wales, and the future Edward VII was one of the finest examples. By shattering the stuffy formality of his parents' generation, he set new style standards that would define the Edwardian era.

Edward VII was most fastidious in his dress, always in well-polished boots, crisp spats and the white slips that he wore beneath his waistcoats. The proud bearer of a not inconsiderable *embonpoint*, he took to wearing the bottom button of his waistcoat undone, thus starting a sartorial craze which exists to this day. The German Chancellor Prince von Bülow described the Prince as the "uncontested *arbiter elegantiarum*".

EDWARD VII IS SEEN AS THE INVENTOR OF THE PLUS FOUR

This opinion was shared by countless European tailors, who would flock to Marienbad to take clandestine photographs of the Prince in his various outfits, while he took the waters there, supposedly incognito.

Edward VII was one of the first men to popularise the double-breasted "reefer" jacket, the ancestor of today's double-breasted suit jacket and the blazer. Trousers, during Victorian times, had never been pressed with a central crease, until Edward fell from his horse one day and was rescued by a woodsman. While Edward rested in the woodsman's cottage, his wife took great care in pressing his trousers, adding a crease that Edward took such a liking to that he maintained it thereafter.

The King is seen as the inventor of the plus four. A great tweed lover, he was nevertheless too portly to wear breeches flatteringly, choosing instead to wear the newly introduced Knickerbocker breeches for shooting. He had them cut looser over the knee rather than tapered, thus creating the look closely followed by his grandson. Another of Edward VII's sartorial innovations was the adoption of the bowler hat for informal occasions; not content with black ones, he was responsible for the creation of grey, brown and even white bowlers.

2. FORMALITY

"A gentleman is a man who uses a butter knife when dining alone."

GERALD JENKINS

The City Gent

He used to be the bastion of Britain, sorting the nation's finances out during the week then shooting pheasant at weekends on his estate in Berkshire. These days the city gent has moved rather swiftly to being the country's favourite pariah, and is forced to wear his beloved pin striped suits and bowlers only at night in select gentlemen's clubs, to avoid being stoned in the street.

HABITAT

The City of London, but in standard Essex-boy mufti, to avoid standing out from the crowd.

FEEDING

In the good old days it was slap-up lunches costing the earth; now he has to be seen scurrying back to the office with a sandwich. Naturally the delivery from Les Trois Garcons comes to the back door and the sandwich is binned.

MATING

City gents often confuse mating with sexual harassment. After the office party they are surprised to find themselves in a tribunal, when they fully expected to be proposing marriage.

MIGRATION

Many City gents have recently been forced to migrate due to redundancies, though handsome severance packages have only forced them as far as the Bahamas.

Formal Chaps

The rules for male formal wear are so clear and simple that it's really surprising anyone ever gets it wrong. This gentleman is wearing black tie, yet he sports white gloves – which accompany white tie. He is also wearing a top hat – ditto.

Sunglasses should not really be worn at all with formal wear, unless, as is evident in this case, in an exceptionally hot climate. Even then, they certainly shouldn't resemble flying goggles. And why is everyone looking so miserable? It isn't as if anyone's died.

Now this is nearer the mark. This chap has got his white tie kit all correct, with a well-knotted bow tie and the right degree of crispness to the boiled-front shirt. The addition of a white silk scarf is a nice touch. The only disappointment is the pipe – which is clearly a day pipe and not a dress pipe.

Again, this young fellow's outfit is all of a muddle: white gloves with black tie and so forth. On a positive note, he has managed to come up with a rather eccentric and unique fob for his pocket watch; although Brummell would have choked on his hock and seltzer at the display of more than two links in the watch chain.

Formal Chaps

Sebastian Rücker's taut missive reads: "I am a "Herr". Please be so kind as to enlighten me: Did I accidentally trip and fall in the "Chap" category?" Madam, confusion about your sex is not something we can help you with, for our dictats are purely sartorial – though we can help you with your grammar: you should have said "I am a she." The monocle is good, though, and it's lucky you are flat-chested.

"This is me heading for a night of Gershwin at the Theatre," writes Bob MacDonald.

Presumably you mean provincial rather than West End? No decent theatre within five miles of Shaftesbury Avenue would let you in wearing a country waistcoat with a zoot suit and a fedora. And brown shoes? Must have been either an avant-garde theatre or pantomime.

Bob Shanks tried to do our job for us: "This is an all round good egg. A gentleman who appreciates taking his lady to town for scones & sherry." Well, it isn't quite what the Chap would have said. Still, at least you have the decency to hide under the stairs where no-one will see you. And as for your hideous décor... on the plus side, your lady friend had the good taste to co-ordinate her nail varnish with your eyeballs.

William Smith

Will Smith is a bespoke tailor who trained at Huntsman of Savile Row, first as a coatmaker, then as a pattern cutter. After six years there, he moved to Timothy Everest, where he worked as a pattern cutter for three years and now works as a freelance tailor in Mr. Everest's Spitalfields workshop.

Mr. Smith has always been interested in the 'golden era of style', and dresses accordingly. His presence at one of the multitude of vintage events rooted in the 1930s and 40s, an impeccably attired female equivalent on his arm, always adds tone to the occasion. Mr. Smith pursues his craft with a passion and fervour that is commendable, and he is an elegant champion for the survival of British bespoke tailoring, under the formidable might of factory-produced nylon schmutter ever prevalent on our city's streets.

"I WOULD HAVE THOUGHT IT IS A FAR BETTER THING THAT PEOPLE ARE WEARING SMARTER, MORE WELL-THOUGHT OUT CLOTHING THAN THE USUAL MAN-MADE HIGHLY BRANDED CLOTHING. THE MORE SMARTLY DRESSED PEOPLE, THE BETTER FOR THE REVOLUTION!"

Dinner Jacket

Until 1860, gentlemen attending formal occasions would always have worn a black tailcoat. Then Henry Poole & Co. created a short smoking jacket for the Prince of Wales (later Edward VII) to wear to informal dinner parties as an alternative to white tie. Sartorial rules were undergoing a slight relaxation in the Prince's circle – even lounge suits were being permitted in the country, and the idea of the short smoking jacket was to create a more formal version of the lounge suit, to wear at dinners out of town.

In the spring of 1886, a rich New Yorker named James Potter was a guest of the Prince at Sandringham. Potter admired the Prince's dinner jacket and asked for a recommendation. He was sent to Henry Poole & Co., and returned to New York proudly bearing his new royally approved acquisition. Potter was one of the founders of Tuxedo Park, an exclusive club on the outskirts of New York. At the Tuxedo Club's first Autumn Ball, in October 1886, Griswold Lorillard and his friends turned up in prototype dinner jackets with scarlet satin lapels. There are those who claim that they were essentially wearing tailcoats with the tails cut off and that the Prince of Wales was the true originator of the dinner jacket. Since then a healthy if rather tedious spat has continued over whether the English or the Americans invented the dinner jacket. This was somewhat simplified when the Americans began calling it a "tuxedo" while on this side of the pond we stuck to "dinner jacket". They are now of course identical – although it would be very rare to find an Englishman wearing a DJ with scarlet lapels.

Dinner jackets should always be midnight blue, which colour appears as black under artificial light. They should have peaked satin lapels, whether double or single breasted, and most importantly should not be worn with a cummerbund.

The Dress Shirt

It is the decorative or starched front of dress shirts that distinguishes them from ordinary day shirts. From the early 18th century onwards, lace and frills on gentlemen's shirts grew in popularity and flamboyance, until eventually this look was sullied by association with the ghastly business of the French Revolution. Brummell began to make a virtue of appearing at Regency soirees not just immaculately dressed, but clean – rather than simply masking his man-scent with expensive perfumes, as was the rage among his male peers.

The more restrained, but elegant, pleated bib front then grew in popularity and complexity, following the age-old rule that the more ostensibly simple a garment, the more difficult and expensive it had to be both to make and maintain. Around 1860, starch was employed as the next weapon in asserting class distinction. The bib fronts of the shirts were immersed in starch so thick that the shirts could stand up by themselves, and their separate collars followed suit. Special machines were devised to flatten, polish and shape the starched linen. These machines are still in use today but only in England, as the Americans never mastered starching and resorted instead to processes involving prototype plastics.

> AROUND 1860, STARCH WAS EMPLOYED AS THE NEXT WEAPON IN ASSERTING CLASS DISTINCTION

Laundering these shirts involved boiling them, to remove the starch, bequeathing us the phrase, "boiled shirts". By the early 20th century, the unfortunate demise of the servant class meant that a less labour intensive alternative was created with the "Marcella" or "pique" front

shirt. These maintained some pretence of a stiff bib but could be laundered with considerably less effort.

Modern dress shirts frequently affect a mixture of every historic detail, including the frill, the pleat and the stiffened bib. All tend to be fastened with dress studs rather then the common button. Boiled-front shirts are actually too inflexible for buttons to be practical, so the screw stud has to be employed. While this is not necessary with softer shirts, dress studs are still used, since their time-consuming fastening – best executed by a valet – transports the wearer back to happier, more indulgent times.

John Ruskin

John Ruskin is often portrayed as a rather dull, avuncular figure set against the wild, bohemian Pre-Raphaelite Brotherhood. But if we take a closer look at his wardrobe, we see that Ruskin was the true innovator – as well as creating a look that he stuck to for the best part of his life.

By his early twenties, Ruskin had settled into an outfit that he wore almost consistently until old age. This was a dark blue frock coat with a velvet collar, worn with a bright Oxford-blue stock, black trousers and patent slippers. The blue cravats came from Geohegan of Regent Street, while Ruskin had his suits made at Stultz & Co., the fashionable tailor of Clifford Street. His boots came from Hoby & Co. of Pall Mall, their quality moving him to serenade them in one of his essays, on the watercolourist Edward Clayton: "He is a man of dew. His sketches breathe of morning air, and his grass would wet your feet if you were to walk on it in Hoby's best."

RUSKIN CREATED HIS OWN SUBTLE VARIATION ON THE STANDARD DRESS OF THE DAY

In the true Brummellian sense, Ruskin was a dandy. He created his own subtle variation on the standard dress of the day, setting a style that was copied religiously by university students. The academic establishment was described by the folklorist Sabine Baring Gould as having gone "Ruskin-mad", referring to the sudden craze for wearing coloured ties and stocks rather than black.

But when fashions moved on to some new aesthetic acolyte such as Wilde, Ruskin remained steady on his course. He quietly replaced his frock coats, blue cravats and patent slippers for the next fifty years, probably at the same tailoring establishments. By his late seventies he had progressed from being a sartorial innovator to an eccentric anachronism, yet wearing exactly the same clothes. In 1878, when Ruskin was beginning to suffer from the mental illness that dogged his later life, Canon Scott Holland described him as resembling "something between an old-fashioned nobleman of the forties and an angel that had lost its way."

Cary Grant

Cary Grant was one of the first famous men of the 1940s to stop wearing a hat. It would be another twenty years before JFK finally got the men of the world to do away with hats altogether, but Grant's reasons were more personal: they just didn't suit him. For a man so indelibly associated with style, elegance and grace, Grant was a bundle of hidden neuroses. First the hats had to go, and then there was his size 17-and-a-half neck, earned while performing the strenuous acrobatics of his childhood career. Grant was notoriously self-conscious about it, and eagle-eyed directors like Alfred Hitchcock politely avoided lingering on a rear shot of their star for too long. Grant himself dealt with what he saw as a problem by never wearing an open-necked shirt or a crew-neck sweater. Even in To Catch a Thief, he carries off the resort-casual nautical style by adding a foulard neckerchief.

Cary Grant had accounts with the best London tailors, all of whom were masters of disguising far greater deformities than a slightly larger-than-average collar size. Kilgour, French & Stanbury made his suits, adjusting the shoulders and armholes to balance his silhouette, and adding two side vents (in a decade when the fashion was no vents) so that Grant could put his hand in his pocket without crumpling the coat. Tom Wolfe, a bit of a dandy himself (if a little frozen in 1980s preppy aspic for some tastes), once met Grant for an interview and described his clothes as "all worsteds, broadcloths and silks, all rich and underplayed, like a viola ensemble."

This was the essence of the Grant wardrobe: effortless, simple and classic, with no frills or furbelows. As well as hats, he ditched bow ties early in his career and stuck mainly to plain narrow ties, which came to define his image. His look had nothing to do with commissioning tailors to create it for him; Grant could be just as stylish in an off-the-peg Brooks Brothers coat or a pair of pyjamas. Unlike Bogart, or Astaire, or Noel Coward, one cannot 'dress up' as Cary Grant. Only he could do that. "Everybody wants to be Cary Grant," he once said. "Even I want to be Cary Grant."

"EVEN I WANT TO BE
CARY GRANT"

3. DANDYISM

"The thing that really makes a Dandy is
independence. Otherwise there would be a
set of rules on how to be a Dandy,
and there is no such thing."
JULES BARBEY D'AUREVILLY

The Dandy

This **swaggering boulevardier** lives for nothing other than to dress exquisitely. Most of his clothes are bespoke, apart from a few priceless antique items that he has stolen from the dressing rooms of princes. He is a contradictory creature, in that he desperately craves attention, yet considers his outfit a complete failure if a member of the public compliments him on it.

HABITAT

Any city that has a branch of Tiffany, though the dandy will never go anywhere near it. It is simply somewhere to send admirers who want to buy him presents.

FEEDING

Beau Brummell claimed that he "once ate a pea" and this reflects the dandy approach to dining. He will be too busy being witty at the luncheon table to actually eat anything – and also likely to be wearing a waistcoat so tight that a single pea would burst the buttons.

MATING

Dandies are far too busy getting their cravat knots just right to bother with romance. They see the true object of their desire every day in the mirror – though the attraction is purely physical.

MIGRATION

Dandies do not travel well, as a creased neckerchief during transit is likely to spoil any holiday. In the summer, they may move to a slightly cooler part of the house, but generally prefer not to depart from their chosen postcode.

Eccentric Chaps

In appraising the eccentric, one is constantly searching for authenticity. This man's crumpled shirt and poorly kempt moustache show a certain nonchalance with regards to personal hygiene. Added to the fact that his bow-tie seems to have been tied rather than clipped on, we can conclude that he is genuinely eccentric, though possessing no sartorial flair whatsoever.

Whereas this fellow has simply dressed up as an eccentric and attended a county steam fair, surely one of the most uneccentric activities there is? Real eccentrics play polo with monkeys at the top of Mount Everest and juggle dwarves in the nude, that sort of thing.

He has also mistakenly done up the bottom button of the section of carpet he is wearing as a jacket.

Inventors and scientific boffin types should look like Professor Calculus from the *Tintin* books, rather than presenters from *Top Gear*.

Trying-too-hard Chaps

"I recently had my stag do," writes Richard Walden, "and we had a chap themed weekend."
No you didn't.

While not strictly in fancy dress, 'Commander' James P. Renwick RNR lacks a certain authenticity. There are enough tacky postcards of London available without dressing up like one.

"Chaps," according to Carl Portman, "wear dickies and roses and play chess. All I need now is for you to confirm it. Checkmate!"

Indeed, some Chaps do wear bow ties and buttonholes and play the noble game of chess. Chaps do not, however, fly the St. George's flag anywhere but on their horses when riding into battle; they certainly do not fly it on their cufflinks, their lapels or their neckwear.

Maloviere

Though he resembles a figure glimpsed in the background of a painting by Van Eyck, Maloviere lives and breathes, unbelievably, in the same contemporary world as Kerry Katona. He describes himself as an "actor, calligrapher and astrological therapist", which is perfect for a dandy since it implies that he has never harboured anything as vulgar as a vocation.

Maloviere's dress sense is inspired by historical figures ranging from Charles I to Lytton Strachey. He has all his clothes made either by theatrical costumiers or by tailors based on historical patterns. If an item of clothing wears out, he simply has it copied and continues wearing it. He has not shaved nor had his hair cut short for 30 years. Maloviere is blessed with an extremely svelte figure for his 52 years, and claims still to wear items that were made for him when he was 18.

"THE PROCREATIVE ACT, IN MOST SUPERIOR HOMINID PRIMATES, MAY MORE EFFICACIOUSLY AND PERHAPS APPROPRIATELY BE ACCOMPLISHED IN THE ABSENCE OF, OR AT ALL EVENTS WITHOUT THE UNWARRANTED ADDITION OF, A WAISTCOAT"

Trousers

Not unlike amphibians crawling out of the primeval slime, in about 1760 men began to evolve out of various forms of leg covering that can politely be described as being "skirt-like" and certainly primitive. Breeches became the norm, worn from the waist to the knee with stockings covering the rest of the leg. It was of course Beau Brummell who made the first step out of britches into pantaloons. He didn't like the broken line under the knee of britches, so had his tailor construct a pair that went all the way down to his ankles, requesting the addition of a foot strap to avoid creases and keep the trousers tight and smooth on the leg.

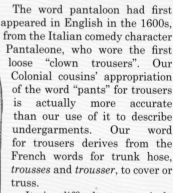

The word pantaloon had first appeared in English in the 1600s, from the Italian comedy character Pantaleone, who wore the first loose "clown trousers". Our Colonial cousins' appropriation of the word "pants" for trousers is actually more accurate than our use of it to describe undergarments. Our word for trousers derives from the French words for trunk hose, *trousses* and *trousser*, to cover or truss.

It is difficult to precisely date when man first walked upright in a pair of trousers rather than pantaloons, but we do know that it was not a painless process. The Duke of Wellington had already come unstuck a century earlier when trying to enter Almacks Club in trousers; this was because trousers were seen as the

IT IS DIFFICULT TO PRECISELY DATE WHEN MAN FIRST WALKED UPRIGHT IN A PAIR OF TROUSERS RATHER THAN PANTALOONS, BUT WE DO KNOW THAT IT WAS NOT A PAINLESS PROCESS

working raiment of sailors, and Wellington should have been in britches.

But by the early 1890s, when trousers had been fully accepted as suitable legwear for men, there were still caveats. Country trousers were frequently rolled up to keep mud off the hems, and a few vanguard tailors tried building the turn-up into the finished trouser. But when Viscount Lewisham entered the House of Commons in 1893 sporting a pair of trousers with turn-ups, there was universal uproar. Turn-ups remained a fixture on trousers until the mid-1920s, when the widening girth of Oxford bags made them impractical. 1925 was a particularly hot summer, and following the example of aesthete Harold Acton, soon everyone in Oxford was wearing trousers with dimensions that reached a preposterous 40 inches.

Austerity measures put paid to such fabric fripperies during the Second World War when anything considered unnecessary, such as trouser turn-ups and waistcoats, was dispensed with, to save on cloth quantities. Turn-ups did not return until the 1950s, and the waistcoat never really came back properly at all.

The Umbrella

In 1936, a newspaper photographer snapped Edward VIII strolling along on a rainy afternoon under an umbrella. The picture caused outrage among the Establishment: carrying a furled umbrella was one thing, but actually opening it was quite *infra dig*: "A gentleman should keep his umbrella tightly furled at all times; in the event of rain, one used it to hail a taxicab."

When umbrellas were first introduced into England in the 18th century by Jonas Hanway, coachmen thought these new-fangled devices would put them out of business, but they needn't have feared. English gents viewed them as effeminate and, if they had them at all, kept them so tightly furled as to resemble walking canes, leaving the ladies to display the latest designs on their canopies. The umbrella's principal function was to maintain a dignified velocity on one's morning stroll, and there is no reason to discontinue observing this tradition: notice the amount of taps that strike the pavement as you swing the brolly alongside your leg – if one tap does not fall precisely between every second footstep, you are walking too fast.

It took the invention of a more reliable frame than whalebone to turn the umbrella into a proper gentleman's accessory. Samuel Fox patented a steel-ribbed frame in 1873, and the Fox Frame is still used today in the construction of high-quality umbrellas. The coated spokes are unmistakable and will provide far more inner strength than one of those absurd "telescopic" umbrellas. You wouldn't buy a telescopic hat or a telescopic pair of trousers (or perhaps you would?), so there is no reason to compromise the shaft of something with a far more complicated construction. Spring-loaded umbrellas are another novelty still with us since the 1960s, and a classic example of technology making our lives more, rather than less, complicated.

IN THE EVENT OF RAIN, ONE USED IT TO HAIL A TAXICAB

The fight between man and umbrella, such a typical sight during heavy showers, is all down to faulty mechanisms. A fellow with a Fox Frame umbrella never has any trouble unfurling it.

Umbrellas have come a long way from the days of Edward VIII, but being permitted to actually use them is as far down the path of progress that one would wish to travel.

Bunny Roger

Often described as the last of his kind, Neil "Bunny" Roger spearheaded a group of ex-Guards officers who spent much of their time loafing about in Savile Row and St James's in the late 1940s. They were dubbed the New Edwardians, young officers just back from the Second World War who found themselves in an England with little patience for frivolity, dandyism or snobbery. They decided collectively to make a flamboyant exit.

Having studied tailoring at Fortnum & Mason, Bunny Roger took a commission in the Rifle Brigade, serving with distinction in Italy and North Africa (but not before making some alterations to the uniform, taking in the dark green trousers until they were as narrow as ballet tights). After being demobbed he set up his own tailoring business in Bruton Mews, before being invited to run the couture department at Fortnum's.

While on holiday on Capri in 1949, Bunny invented the tight-cut trousers which then became a Riviera staple. He went on to single-handedly create the New Edwardian look. This involved radically cut suits with narrow waists, high shoulders and extremely tight waistcoats. His colour palette veered away from Savile Row tradition, with suits in purple, bottle green and ruby red. Bunny Roger's waistcoats were described as "sausage skins", and he complemented the look with curly-brimmed bowlers, monocles, three-quarter length double-breasted covert coats and Malacca canes. Even in his 80s, he still cut a lithe figure, and was celebrated for his lavish parties and his energetic dancing.

Long after he had abandoned it, the New Edwardian look was corrupted into the "Teddy Boy" outfit adopted by working class men in the 1950s. They kept the gaudy palette but found cheaper East-End tailors and replaced the bowlers with greasy DA hairstyles. They did not wear monocles.

EVEN IN HIS 80S, HE WAS CELEBRATED FOR HIS
LAVISH PARTIES AND HIS ENERGETIC DANCING

4. CADDERY

"He is every other inch a gentleman."
REBECCA WEST

The Cad

Obviously, the cad approach is an entire philosophy rather than a dress code, but a true bounder will rarely be scruffy, for that would make him a mere rotter. Cads use clothes to attract the ladies, so their wardrobe is quite showy, veering on the kitsch, but rarely the vulgar. This means cravats rather than ties, blazers and flannels rather than suits, co-respondent shoes rather than brogues.

HABITAT

Terrace cafés on the Riviera, the lobbies of 5-star hotels in cities such as Cairo, Budapest and Buenos Aires. Bounders have largely been driven out of their former habitat – English seaside towns – by their predators, Angry Husbands.

FEEDING

Cads are far more interested in the ladies at other tables in restaurants than the bill of fare. A brace of oysters every two days forms part of the seduction ritual, and also keeps their figures svelte as they descend into middle age.

MATING

It's all they do.

MIGRATION

Cads head south when the British winter sets in, as ladies' winter garments display nothing of any interest for them to look at.

Cads

At first glance there is nothing to complain about here. This man has clearly seen a Terry-Thomas film or twain, has made an effort to adorn his upper lip and perhaps has some nefarious plans with a filly. But wait a moment... what at first could have been taken for a cravat turns out to be a T-shirt; he isn't wearing a straw boater to go with his blazer...and is that a bottle of champagne, or...Heaven help him – it's Cava.

This chap is such a bounder (and a French one to boot) that he has hidden his lady friend's clothing, forcing her to slip on a pair of curtains and a dog to hide her modesty. Tanguy himself, meanwhile, got his orders to his tailor and to his upholsterer mixed up, resulting in this sartorial abomination.

"Some say I look like a young Pierce Brosnan," writes Michael Brownsell. "What do you think, chaps?"

According to Chappist evolutionary theory, a young Pierce Brosnan would be Roger Moore; an even younger one Sean Connery. You look like neither. However, you would make a thoroughly convincing Bond villain.

Chaps with Whiskers

"I present for your delectation," writes Will Ball, "a picture taken of myself whilst taking part in the recent 'Tweed Run' cycling event."

Why? I mean, why do any of this? Why throw on a mélange of clothes that bear no relation to each other, either via fabrics, colours or historical references, and none of which fit you. Why grow whiskers when you have no intention of dressing accordingly (in the clothing of an Edwardian gentleman, for example). Lastly, what is that thing on your head? Some sort of tweed condom?

Martin Hobby's excuse for this moustache is that he grew it while nursing a broken foot at home. Admittedly there is nothing wrong with the lip weasel itself – but why go to all that trouble only to spoil it with a cardboard bowler, an ugly dressing gown and a revolting pair of spectacles? And as for not shaving before having your picture taken – shame on you sir!

Michael "Atters" Attree

Atters is best known for his luxuriant handlebar moustac and his reputation as a bit of a bounder. But he is at pains point out that he is much more than "just a lip weasel". (Desp being Chairman and Honourable Master of Ceremonies at t World Beard & Moustache Championships, Brighton 2007).

Atters' interest in the paranormal knows no bounds, and regularly drifts through walls to prove it (though usually the ti of the tache hold him back from a complete astral projection). regularly performs a one-moustache (sorry, one-man) show call Atters Attree's Chaporgasmic Terrors, in which he demonstrat his research into paranormal activity and conspiracy theories.

The performances are accompanied by live Theremin and t gradual removal of women's clothing, receiving mixed recepti from the audience. In Ireland, Atters' lecture on a 'lactatir Nefertiti and The Pope's 'PayPal Stigmata' saw the poor fell booed off stage and a sheep's heart was thrown at him.

This seems a bit unfair, considering his tireless work for t less fortunate. While living on the Island of Iona, for examp Atters founded the world's first ladies-only pipe smoking club the monastery. When complaints began to trickle in about l attempts to re-enact key scenes from The Wicker Man, Atters w proud to note that "an ecclesiastical invitation to leave the isla duly arrived".

"GOD I LOVE HIS MOUSTACHE.

IS IT REAL?"

(FELLOW BOUNDER LESLIE PHILIPS

ON ATTERS)

The Cravat

The word **cravat derives originally** from the word "Croat". During the reign of Louis XIII, the French army boasted a cavalry regiment composed exclusively of Croats, called Royal-Cravate. The French, with a keen eye for any new fashion accessory, soon adopted the Croat officers' neckwear. This was a length of common lace, with the ends arranged *en rosette* or ornamented with a button or tuft, which hung gracefully on the breast. This new arrangement was at first termed a Croat, then corrupted to Cravate in French. This has led to much confusion, since in French *cravate* now means necktie, while they call a cravat a *foulard*.

> THE CRAVAT GAVE GENTLEMEN WITH LOUCHE TENDENCIES ACCESS TO THE LOVELY LADIES INHABITING THE WORLD OF "FLOWER POWER"

By the early 19th century, the cravat had evolved, throughout Europe, into the stock. Once the macaronis started wearing them, their size grew to flamboyant proportions. By the time of Brummell, shirt collars were as high as the tips of the ears, and the cravat was a complicated ensemble, partly covering the mouth in some cases, which could only be tied with assistance. Witness Brummell's valet, commenting to a visitor as he deposited yet more piles of starched cravats outside his master's dressing room: "These, sir, are our failures." Once assembled, the wearer would have difficulty turning his head, and would march about St James's with his face fixed directly ahead of him.

The Victorians, always quick to snuff out any flamboyance, soon replaced the cravat with the necktie, and it did not reappear until the relative relaxation of dress codes in the 1930s. During the Second World War the cravat came into its own, having migrated from the outside of the shirt collar to the inside, where it provided a useful protection from the itchy serge of British uniforms.

By the 1960s the cravat was enjoying a full renaissance, albeit in its baser form inside the shirt collar. The cravat, in allowing the wearer to be properly attired but with his shirt collar open, gave gentlemen with louche tendencies access to the lovely ladies inhabiting the world of "flower power". It ultimately became the symbol of a cad, personified by a winking Leslie Phillips in flannels, blazer, pencil moustache and a triangle of paisley at his throat. The cravat is also used effectively to signify the wrongdoings of David Niven's character in Terrence Rattigan's *Separate Tables*. All the other gentlemen appear at breakfast wearing ties.

Spats

L et us not confuse spats with Gaiters, which are worn over the shoe and lower trouser leg, primarily in a protective capacity. Spats are purely decorative, though their name comes from 'spatterdash' and they were meant to dash the spatter of mud on one's trousers. Spats were first worn by the military around 1878 and were soon adopted by Victorian gentlemen to wear with a frock coat. French infantry wore white spats for parade and off-duty wear until 1903. Italian soldiers wore light tan spats until 1910 and the Japanese Army wore long white spats during the Russo-Japanese War of 1905. Today, the Royal Regiment of Scotland, into which all Scottish line infantry regiments were amalgamated in 2006, retains white spats as part of its uniform.

In 1923 King George V opened the Chelsea Flower Show in a frock coat, grey top hat and spats. In 1926 he opened the same event in a morning coat, grey top hat but no spats. The bushes were said to be littered with discarded spats that day, as gentlemen furiously discarded them in honour of the King. In one fell swoop King George had created morning dress, little changed to this day. Spats were rarely seen outside of music halls in Britain after that, but across the Atlantic they carried on regardless.

> EVEN WHEN CRIMINALS WORE SPATS, IT WAS USUALLY WITH A MORNING SUIT – IN THOSE DAYS ONE WOULDN'T CONSIDER MURDERING SOMEONE IN THE WRONG CLOTHES

Charlie Chaplin wore them when off-duty, as did Fred Astaire, Irving Berlin and Duke Ellington. But it wasn't only the good guys: spats were also worn by Al Capone, and fictional gangsters often wore them, such as Spats Colombo, played by George Raft in *Some Like it Hot*. Mack the Knife, played by Rudolf Forster, also wears them to greatly sinister effect in the film of *The Threepenny Opera*.

Even when criminals wore them, it was usually with a morning suit – in those days one wouldn't consider murdering someone in the wrong clothes. Brown spats are rare beasts indeed; they either came in white linen (for the summer) or dove-grey canvas (for the winter). A line of pearl buttons often fastened the spats at the side. Men who wore spats in the 1930s with a tailored waistcoat were known as purveyors of the 'Boulevard Style'.

By the mid-1940s spats had, for the most part, disappeared from the fashion scene, replaced by rubber galoshes, which did a much better job of keeping feet warm and dry.

Terry-Thomas

If a distinction can be made between a cad and a bounder, it could be made along sartorial lines. A bounder is usually more flamboyantly dressed than a cad – whose womanizing is slightly more underhand than a bounder's. If the accepted crown of English caddery is held by Leslie Phillips, the garland for über-bounder must surely go to Terry-Thomas.

Even as a child, the young Thomas Terry Hoar Stevens felt he had been the victim of a genetic mix-up when he was born into North Finchley of a father who worked at Smithfield meat market. Persuaded to enter his father's profession, the 16-year-old T-T turned up on his first day in a taupe double-breasted suit with a carnation, a green pork pie hat and yellow kid gloves, twirling a silver-topped Malacca cane. It was, he would later recall, "the first, fine, florid rapture" of his adult dandyism.

In the army, T-T insisted on wearing brown suede shoes with his Khakis – a colour reserved for officers, which he was not. He even persuaded former tailors in his regiment to run him up a bespoke battle dress based on his own design. With his elongated whangee cigarette holder, he cut such a dash in the entertainment corps that he was regularly saluted as an officer.

It wasn't long before his true calling beckoned, and T-T quickly rose through the ranks of comedy roles in radio, television and film, eventually establishing himself in Hollywood as the archetypal English upper class twit. He dressed accordingly in real life and even managed to iron all the Finchley out of his accent.

Terry-Thomas's was not a maverick wardrobe, but it did contain a few individual flourishes. Offset against some 80 bespoke suits were 150 of his trademark fancy waistcoats, both double- and single-breasted and fashioned of every conceivable fabric from red velvet to mink (yes, this does sound a tad vulgar – but the latter was made especially for the premiere of *Make Mine Mink* in 1960). He always had the breast pockets on his suits cut seven inches deep, to accommodate his cigarette holders, and he never left the house without a clove carnation buttonhole, even if he were simply popping out to the pub.

5. DARKNESS

"Why am I so beautiful but so
obsessed with doom?"
SEBASTIAN HORSLEY

The Libertine

There is a little of the Libertine in all chaps, and in a way he lives out the unfulfilled fantasies of men too scared to delve into the darkness. We would rather get a thrill from reading about our velvet-clad counterpart getting in trouble with the beak again than actually set foot in an opium den/bordello/nail bar. Libertines are the only chaps who dabble with make-up, and let's keep it that way, shall we?

HABITAT

A flat in the deprived area of a capital city where people are always screaming outside.

FEEDING

The libertine gets all his sustenance from wine, laudanum and the occasional glass of blood (on Sundays and special occasions).

MATING

He casually mates at odd hours of the day, with odd creatures who are not necessarily equipped to procreate.

MIGRATION

The Libertine rarely takes holidays, apart from the occasional visit to Transylvania to frighten the locals.

Weirdo Chaps

"These pictures originated on a rather jolly evening involving some light refreshments in our academic club house," writes Nikolas Westphal, a Doctoral Candidate at the Leipzig Graduate School of Management.

Sir, you are wearing jeans, you are German and there is a man's face in your crotch. The question as to whether you are a Chap or not is entirely irrelevant.

"My rugby club recently had a 'retro' awards night," writes Rob Nichol, "and I tried to finally embrace the chap which has been growing inside me since discovering your fine publication."

At first I didn't know what he was talking about. Then I saw the expression on Rob's face and knew exactly what he meant by "the chap which has been growing inside me".

"Whenever I meet someone new," writes Frank Hull, "I always take a look at their shoes, fingernails, hair, watch and the cut of their clothes. You can tell a lot about a person just from these things, as well as their manners of course. I may only be a 33-year-old man, but I was brought up with old fashioned Catholic morals and values and I'm yet to meet a young lady with similar values."

Is this any surprise, given that you have the air of someone who has just hidden his grandmother's corpse in the bushes?

One glance at this fellow's face and we simply know that he believes that highly intelligent lizards live and breathe among us, waiting to conquer the world. Even more disturbing is his belief that it is acceptable to unfasten two buttons on one's shirt when wearing a cravat.

Mark Powell

Bespoke tailors who dress as well as their clients are few and far between. They are usually background figures happy to watch their clients saunter out of the shop to dazzle the world with the tailor's creations.

Not so Mark Powell. His entire collection is based around his own personal look – which contains something of the wartime spiv, a touch of the zoot-suited black jazz musician from the 1930s and aspects of the New Edwardians or early teddy boys. Powell has chosen Soho, rather than Savile Row, to ply his trade for the last 25 years, partly because he is too much of a maverick to blend in with the Row's old guard, but principally because Soho suits him, his world and his clients – who range from local pop musicians to gangland bosses.

Rather reassuringly for a maverick, he refers to himself in the third person: "If a client wants Mark Powell to give them the ideal style, I'm very good at interpreting what people want." This habit gives him a slightly menacing air, which, coupled with the way he twirls his cutting shears around and snaps his tape measure, makes him the sort of tailor whom one doesn't argue with about turned-back cuffs or pocket linings.

"I ALWAYS WEAR A SUIT WITH A TIE; I NEVER WEAR A SUIT WITH A SHIRT UNBUTTONED AT THE TOP. THAT'S ONE OF THE WORST THINGS TO HAPPEN IN STYLING IN RECENT TIMES – THAT RELAXED LOOK"

The Walking Cane

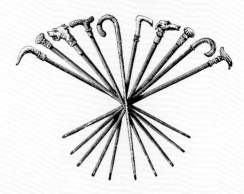

Walking canes first came into fashion around the end of the 17th century. The bewildering variety of styles reflects their purpose: a gnarled, robust stick with a head made from an antler will serve you in the country, while a narrower stick made from ebony with a silver top will cut more of a dash in town.

In the walking cane's sartorial peak, the late Victorian era, they came to denote a man's professional status: medical men would have a cane with a coiled serpent around the head, while members of the aristocracy's canes would bear their crest embossed into the gold head. Much lower down the social scale were the scrimshaw canes, carved by whalers out of chunks of whalebone and decorated with nautical scenes and sexual fantasies. Ironically, these now command vast sums at auction.

> THE MOST
> UNUSUAL
> ANIMAL CANE
> IS THE BULL
> PIZZLE

Victorian gentlemen were much prone to attack from footpads and ruffians, and soon learned to use their walking canes to great advantage. First came the swordstick, with a two-foot blade concealed in the shaft. Then there was the stiletto, often used by pimps to protect their professional charges. A five-inch blade emerged from the head when the cane was flicked against the forearm. A gentleman traveller named Edward Barton-Wright developed an entire system of self-defence for gentlemen, using canes, sticks and umbrellas, known as Bartitsu, which he based on martial arts he had studied in the orient. Regular classes were held in London and the system even got a mention in the *Adventures of Sherlock Holmes*.

As the Victorians explored the farther reaches of the world, so they discovered new and exotic materials with which to fashion canes. The entire spinal columns of sharks and stingrays were used as canes, filled with an iron rod and filed to a smooth column. The most unusual animal cane is the Bull pizzle. The bull's penis was severed and stretched from a beam until it was some three feet long. Over time it would harden and the top would be decorated with a smoked bull's testicle.

The Top Hat

When London haberdasher John Hetherington set
forth from his rooms in his new, personally designed
top hat in January 1797, he had no idea that he would end
up before the Beak. The sight of his extravagant topper
caused ladies to swoon, children to howl and an errand boy
to break his arm in the ensuing mayhem.

Hetherington was later charged with "occasioning a
breach of the peace by wearing a tall structure having a
shining lustre calculated to frighten timid people." He was
fined £500. Nowadays, you would be lucky to purchase an
original Victorian silk top hat for less than that.

But all Hetherington had done was to create a silk-
covered variant of the common riding hat, which resembled
a top hat but was made from beaver fur and had a wider
brim and a lower crown. Despite initial over-reaction to
Hetherington's silk
topper, by the mid-19th
century they were *de
rigeur* headwear for
everyone from funeral
directors to bankers.

Dandies soon adapted
them so that theirs
towered over everyone
else's with flared
crowns and swooping
brims. The French
dandies, known as *Les
incroyables*, wore top
hats of such outlandish

> DANDIES SOON
> ADAPTED THE TOPPER
> SO THAT THEIRS
> TOWERED OVER
> EVERYONE ELSE'S
> WITH FLARED CROWNS
> AND SWOOPING
> BRIMS

dimensions that there was no room for them in overcrowded
cloakrooms. Along came Antoine Gibus in 1823 and
invented the collapsible opera hat. The American financier
J.P. Morgan took a less practical approach: he ordered a
limousine with an especially high roof so he could ride
around without taking his hat off.

Once Prince Albert showed his approval of the top hat
around 1850, they swiftly became such a part of everyday

life in the city that historian James Laver described an assemblage of toppers as resembling rows of factory chimneys.

The end of top hats in the City coincided with the Big Bang in 1986. Until then, all stockjobbers had worn them to work, but they decided to put them aside in favour of less conspicuous attire. Around the same time, two brothers who owned the last silk plush looms in Lyon had a bit of a to-do, which resulted in the destruction of the 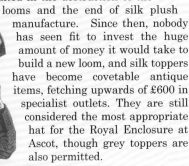 looms and the end of silk plush manufacture. Since then, nobody has seen fit to invest the huge amount of money it would take to build a new loom, and silk toppers have become covetable antique items, fetching upwards of £600 in specialist outlets. They are still considered the most appropriate hat for the Royal Enclosure at Ascot, though grey toppers are also permitted.

Sebastian Horsley

Sebastian Horsley was an Anarcho-dandyist-anachronism, and a beautiful one, to boot. An outrageous Regency fop in an age of bland tracksuits, blond highlights and dull opinions; the very fact that Sebastian endured the 21st century at all was a slap in the face with a scented handkerchief to all that he despised. When he died aged 47, Sebastian still looked like a rock star. People are sometimes described as "lighting up the room". When Sebastian sauntered along Old Compton Street, he lit up the whole of Soho. He commanded the street and sucked all the energy of the Queer Mile towards him, bathing in its sickly neon tint and getting sustenance from it.

Sebastian's dandyism was unique: a completely original work of art. Instead of eyeing up duchesses in carriages on Rotten Row, he followed hookers up grotty alleys in Soho, revelling in the filth and squalor of an anti-life. If invited to an event outside the W1 postcode, he would simply throw the card in the dustbin. This was not a pose or an affectation; this was making a choice and sticking to it.

> THE VERY FACT THAT SEBASTIAN ENDURED THE 21ST CENTURY AT ALL WAS A SLAP IN THE FACE WITH A SCENTED HANDKERCHIEF TO ALL THAT HE DESPISED

Horsley was the last of the English dandies, and he kept dandyism alive for just a few more years. "Dandyism is the last flicker of heroism in decadent ages," wrote Baudelaire. The early years of this century may have been a decadent age, but it was a spiritual rather than a moral decadence: an age of triviality, superficiality and unoriginality, during which one man flared up in a red velvet suit and trampled over everything that was considered important.

The flame has been extinguished. Our world is without heat and full of melancholy.

6. MATURITY

"I attribute my longevity to constant smoking
and marrons glacés."

Nöel Coward

The Old Codger

Unlike the Dandy, this hearty fellow can't wait to tuck into his roast guinea fowl, followed by a mountain of profiteroles. He usually favours some form of facial hair and relies on his tailor to disguise his burgeoning embonpoint. His wardrobe contains row upon row of tweed suits and Tattersall check shirts, and he probably does not own a single pair of swimming trunks.

HABITAT

Either a modest little pile in Shropshire or a town house in Surrey.

FEEDING

Hearty English fare (none of that foreign muck), and the sorts of town restaurants where the food is served from trolleys by elderly waiters.

MATING

The old codger is more interested in pudding than popsies, but occasionally harbours some dark perversion that he pays a young lady in Mayfair to see to once a month.

MIGRATION

The old codger would never travel abroad in search of warmer climes. When it gets cold he simply adds another dog to his bed.

Oldies

Not only did Keith Patterson sign his letter as "Master of the Uxorial Bedchamber", but he also wrote: "May the President of the Immortals, in the Aeschyleaan phrase, continue to smile upon you."

Before even looking at the photograph it was entirely obvious that Mr. Patterson was a Chap.

At first glance, everything seems to be in order here: the ratio of tweed:silk:cotton is satisfactory, the men are bewhiskered and the ladies are not displaying their midriffs.

But – wait a moment. Are they really taking luncheon in a caravan? Oh Good Lord, it gets worse. It also looks as though they bought their victuals in a supermarket.

Nautical Chaps

"This picture was taken this summer while embarked upon a grand tour of Europe to celebrate my marriage," writes Simon Kind.

The Chap has always prided itself on its lack of discrimination towards the disabled. This fellow has done his best to dress appropriately for a stroll on deck, and his wardrobe clearly contains some first-class items of apparel. It is a tragedy for all concerned, however, not least his blushing bride, that Mr. Kind's blindness has resulted in his donning a pair of formal braces with linen trousers!

Sam V. Aldred didn't get very far in convincing anybody he was in the Royal Navy. A Lieutenant would never wear his life vest under his coat, neither would he wear school trousers with mess kit.

But the real giveaway is the use of a brown sock on the smoke alarm. An officer in the Senior Service would only ever apply a black sock to such a purpose.

Nautical Chaps

The Royal Navy used to have rules about facial hair. A full set was mandatory for all officers, and Anton seems to have got this right. Where he went wrong, however, was in assuming that he was also required to be in possession of a full set of breasts.

"**C**an a Frenchman fully qualify as a chap?" asks Pierre Gay. Strictly speaking, no. But when you carry off such an air of casual yet refined masculinity, and dress for the poop deck without fuss of furbelows, with the added handicap, at least in nautical circles, of your surname, you are an example to us all (and especially Anton).

Peter Drysdale lives in British Columbia, where he clearly spends a lot of time at home trying on various outfits that remind him of dear old Blighty. With décor like that, I can see no reason to spend any time at home at all. Mr. Drysdale's aesthetic approach is all the more surprising in a state whose motto is "Splendour without Diminishment".

Paul Lawford

Once upon a time, this nation played host to a type of gentleman virtually unknown in other countries – the English eccentric. Until recently, one would spot members of this species dotted about in most of the Home Counties. Their distinguishing features were voluminous facial hair, hats, damaged footwear and a large amount of lapel badges.

Sadly there are few left. The great sportswear deluge of the 1990s virtually wiped all the eccentrics out, but still a few survive. One such is Paul Lawford, one half of electro-folk music combo the Rubbishmen of Soho. Paul lives in a towering bedsit on a dark Soho street, from where one can hear the sound of Bells Whisky bottles being smashed at all hours.

He likes pubs, understandably, and has been barred from most of the ones not worth revisiting. But the heady triumvirate of the French Pub, the Coach and Horses and Gerry's is happy to welcome Mr. Lawford's bulging wallet on a Tuesday morning, when he has just received a cheque from his aged Auntie Mildred. He subsists on a diet of cream cakes and gin, principally for dietary reasons, but also to support ailing British industries. Mr. Lawford has various tailors, according to his requirements. Miss Sue Ryder for overcoats, Mr. Oxfam for the suits and Messrs Salvation & Army for military wear.

"DURING HOT WEATHER I SOMETIMES
OMIT TO WEAR A WAISTCOAT. BUT TO AVOID
OFFENDING ANYONE, I THEN COVER MY
NAKEDNESS WITH A LIGHT OVERCOAT"

The Cloth Cap

The cloth cap can be traced back to the 14th century in Britain and parts of Italy, when it was more likely to be called a bonnet. A 1571 Act of Parliament to stimulate domestic wool consumption decreed that all males over six years old, except for the nobility and persons of degree, were to wear caps of wool manufacture on Sundays and holidays, on force of a fine ¾ pence per day. By the time the Bill was repealed in 1597, the woolen cloth cap had taken its place as a recognisable mark of a commoner.

This lasted until the 19th century, when members of the aristocracy began jealously eyeing up the practical headwear of their estate staff and getting their tailors to run them up similar items, in more expensive materials such as tweed and silk. The flat cap took its place as casual country wear, particularly on the golf course, for the upper classes. The tweed cap remained the most common hat on the links for decades, until the scourge of the American

baseball style cap entirely replaced it in the latter part of the 20th century. In America, the association between flat caps and the working man was cemented by its adoption by news vendors (gaining its moniker of the "Newsboy Cap"), as newspaper and baker boys wore them to make deliveries on their bicycles around London and New York.

The English Baker Boy Cap is made in a similar way to the flat cap, but with a wider crown made from eight panels, stitched together with a button on the top – hence they are often called eight-sectioned caps. Other names for them are: Apple Cap, Jay Gatsby (after The Great Gatsby), Redford Cap, Fisherman's Cap, Lundberg Stetson and a Brooklyn.

Both types of cap have now come full circle and can be worn by gentlemen, although their reputation has been somewhat downgraded through their adoption by hip-hop artistes, who choose to wear them with track suits and plimsolls. Tweed caps should only be worn with tweed suits. The older ones have a deeper back and a longer peak than the modern ones, so it is worth seeking out vintage examples, especially since, unlike felt hats, they rarely lose their original shape.

Harris Tweed

The official definition of Harris Tweed is as follows: "A tweed which has been hand woven by the islanders at their homes in the Outer Hebrides, finished in the islands of Harris, Lewis, North Uist, Benbecula, South Uist and Barra and their several purtenances (The Outer Hebrides) and made from pure virgin wool dyed and spun in the Outer Hebrides."

Harris Tweed is without doubt one of the most beautiful fabrics in the world; it is therefore no surprise that its provenance and manufacture should be so strictly controlled. The Harris Tweed Association was formed in 1906, leading to the establishment of a trademark. Later the Harris Tweed Authority replaced the Association, and standards of this superlative tweed were enshrined in law under the Harris Tweed Act of 1993.

It is comforting when Parliament becomes involved in gentlemen's tailoring, and perhaps reflects the quantity of MPs who used to don tweed garments as soon as they left London every weekend. The colour palette of Harris Tweed reflects the rich colours visible across the Outer Hebrides, making it a staple for upper class country wear since the early 19th century.

It is somewhat ironic that its production has always occurred at the other end of the social spectrum. It is also surprising to learn that the cause of the oddly musty smell given off by a vintage Harris Tweed jacket when it gets damp is human urine.

In the early 1800s, wool from the Western Isles of Scotland was coloured with dyes from local plants and lichens, then processed, spun, and hand-woven by the crofters in their cottages. The final stage of the process was to soak it in human urine, whose ammonia served not only to deepen and intensify the dye colours, but also to remove the oils of melted dogfish livers that had been used to dress the wool.

This was all part of a four-part process known as "waulking", which gave the tweed more body but also shrank it slightly. Waulking was a day-long project and once begun it had to be finished in one session. The result was a bolt of tweed reduced from eight finger lengths wide to a full three inches narrower, making for a much softer, thicker, and more tightly woven fabric.

The process of waulking involved around 12 women pounding the tweed against a board or trampling it with their feet. The process was always accompanied by waulking songs, a musical form unknown elsewhere in Western Europe. The chants are very rhythmic and were composed to keep the beat when the cloth was being waulked. The practice of waulking continued right into the 1950s, so any jacket dated before this time is likely to have been subjected to such intense and archaic production methods.

> ✺
>
> ### IT IS COMFORTING WHEN PARLIAMENT BECOMES INVOLVED IN GENTLEMEN'S TAILORING
>
> ✺

The real credit for the fabulous patterns seen on Harris Tweed to this day rests with Lady Catherine Herbert, wife of the 6th Earl of Dunmore. In 1846 she commissioned two local weavers to create lengths of Tweed in the Murray family tartan. She had the finished fabric made up into tweed jackets for the gamekeepers and ghyllies on her estate. When Lady Catherine's guests remarked on the staff's fabulous jackets, she saw the potential of Harris Tweed as ideal for the country pursuits her set indulged in. Harris Tweed soon became the fabric of choice for the landed gentry, including members of Queen Victoria's inner circle.

As demand increased, Lady Catherine improved the yarn production process to create a more consistent, workable cloth, and by the late 1840s merchants from Edinburgh to London were supplying the privileged classes with hand-woven Harris Tweed.

Today, every 50 metres of genuine Harris Tweed is checked by an inspector from the Harris Tweed Authority before being stamped with its distinctive orb symbol. All tweed jackets made from genuine Harris Tweed carry the orb trademark, as well as a number identifying the weaver of the fabric and the date it was finished in the Outer Hebrides.

7. FOREIGN CLIMES

"Abroad is utterly bloody and all
foreigners are fiends."
NANCY MITFORD

The Colonial Chap

Though not as influential as he used to be, the Colonial Chap still commands respect in certain quarters of the world. Wherever he goes, a large gathering of natives follows, eager to show him the sights and sell him local handicrafts. In some African countries it has even become fashionable for local celebrities to adopt a British child and add him to their extended family. They survive as children, but once they reach adulthood are very unlikely to flourish, deprived of their hourly G&Ts, Vaughan Williams symphonies and Ovaltine.

HABITAT

The British Embassies of places such as Nairobi, Cairo and Dar Es Salaam.

FEEDING

Their aversion to local produce is legendary, and Colonial Chaps would rather live on baked beans and Marmite than anything with spices, garlic or vegetables in it.

MATING

Colonial Chaps are drawn to dark-skinned exotic beauties, but as soon as they have married them, insist on them wearing English-style pinnies, baking scones and learning all the words to "Walter, don't lead me to the Altar."

MIGRATION

Every Christmas they flock to the Embassy for a traditional English Christmas luncheon, to which the natives are not invited; instead they are given a piece of glazed fruit each.

Colonial Chaps

Excellent carriage, elegant clothing, a face bearing aristocratic hauteur, and splendid facial hair: a Chap of the highest order. The fellow on his right is perhaps some sort of factotum. Not a very well paid one, by the looks of his suit.

Charlie Chan makes "no excuse for the use of an American weapon. When one is defending one's pink gin, one must use anything that comes to hand."

Defending it against what? The other poorly dressed guests at some dull suburban barbecue, where drinks are served in plastic beakers?

Torquil Arbuthnot probably thinks he resembles a shifty dealer in saucy postcards on a street corner in Cairo, circa 1937. When in reality he is a semi-retired chiropractor from Cheam on his way to a murder mystery weekend.

Colonial Chaps

Thomas Richard Grenville Wilson explains that he picked up this Italian linen suit from "some fellow on the Charing Cross Road, who altered it to my specifications whilst I spent a couple of hours in the National Portrait Gallery."

Looking at portraits of Norman Wisdom, no doubt. There can be no other explanation for leaving the bottom button of the coat fastened, knotting your tie like a schoolboy, wearing some sort of ghastly tie clip and wearing the low form of fez, rather than the more debonair higher sort. Oh, and not shaving.

Ooh, hello! That's a nice wastepaper basket on your head – did you buy it from a local weaving co-operative? This man's bizarre floral shirt is almost forgivable, given that he is travelling abroad – but what on earth possessed him to pair a white linen suit with *black boots*?

"While awaiting the Indian Mail at Brindisi," writes Edward Snelson-James, "I thought I overheard talk that parts of the Empire had been granted independence."

Yes, they decided they could no longer put up with their colonial overlords' embarrassing attempts at going native. They were also becoming rather nauseated by their swollen feet and ugly wristwatches.

Foreign Chaps

The lady in Horatio Holzbein's painting is having difficulty covering her pink areas, and he has forgotten to unfasten the bottom button on his waistcoat. They must both be French. There can be no other explanation for a tie made out of wallpaper, a coat made of cardboard and trousers made of papier-mâché.

This chap seems to tick all the right boxes, regarding eyewear, neckwear, cuff-wear and position of velvet. So what's the catch? Well, it turns out that Erik P. Löffler is from Continental Europe.

"You may excuse the charmingly nonchalant turnout of Mr. Achleitner (left)," began Nikolas Westphal's pathetic grovelling, "as someone who is by intellect and nature deeply rooted in the swamps of the Germanic fatherland. In my case (right), on the other hand, I hope that panache and stiff upper lip clearly demonstrate the extensive term I was able to spend in Merry Old England."

Frankly no, on both counts.

Foreign Chaps

"I want to believe I am able to be a Chap...Let me know if I am right. My name is Marcus de Saint-Elode and I am French."

Well I think you've answered your own question, monsieur.

"Are there any events, shops or places of interest for me, during my stay in London?" asks Brian JC Osborne, a Cypriot property developer.

Yes. The cutters on Savile Row have promised to horsewhip anyone who dares to walk along the Row in jeans. It would be a pleasure to see you there.

"I am fully clad in the Indian tradition (predating all chaps by about a millennium)," writes Sanjaya Kanoria, "but lacking that most essential, some would aver, sacred thread that is supposed to help a gentleman remain one in the face of evil temptation." What, a cravat? Nevertheless, there is a certain sense of sartorial purity here, despite being practically naked.

Barima Owusu-Nyantekyi

Barima is a writer and fashion consultant who flits between London, Ghana and Hong Kong. He is part of a new generation of youngsters fascinated by classic gentlemen's clothing, and pens one of the better of the multitude of blogs which exists on this particular subject.

Chiming perfectly with the views of The Chap, Barima believes that "men want to step up their game, cast off the teenage garments that have taken many of them far into their 40s, and allow the marketers and designers to steer them towards the classicist world of traditional gentleman's raiment."

With his glamorous lifestyle, Barima has every opportunity to be appalled at the poor standards maintained at events at which dressing up used to be mandatory – the opera, the ballet, the theatre and "red-carpet" events. He has personally witnessed grown men mocking pocket squares, even snatching them out of another man's breast pocket; and tales of young partygoers in America being hassled by their peers for "dressing up" in a shirt and chinos and being asked whether they were "gay or European?"

Barima is impressed by the efforts made by certain American dandies to influence better modes of dress in their fans, to whit Derek Watkins (or Fonzworth Bentley), entertainer and former valet to Sean 'Diddy' Combs; Andre Benjamin (or Andre 3000); Willie Brown (former Mayor of San Francisco). On this side of the Ocean, Barima admires the dress sense of Prince Charles, Gay Talese and Beppe Modenese.

I HAVE ALWAYS BELIEVED THAT BEING WELL
TURNED OUT IS ALL ENCOMPASSING, AND THAT
EVEN THE MOST CASUAL OUTFIT FOR A NIGHT ON
THE TOWN SHOULD HAVE SOME FLAIR

The Panama Hat

The origins of the Panama hat can be traced back to the 16th Century, when the Incas of Ecuador first used the toquilla plant to produce straw hats. They are produced in Ecuador and exported all over the world to this day, so why are they called Panama hats and not Ecuador hats?

From 1848, prospectors heading for the Californian gold fields passed through the Isthmus of Panama, an important centre and staging post for international trade, picking up a hat on their way. All the hats sold in Panama had come from Ecuador, but they came to be known by the name of their point of sale rather than their place of origin. Soon, huge quantities of hats were being exported to California, all of them shipped via Panama. By the time a shrewd Frenchman named Philippe Raimond exhibited the toquilla hats at the 1855 World Fair in Paris, the Panama name was firmly established and was never corrected.

—⁂—

THE BEST QUALITY PANAMA HATS SOLD IN BRITAIN ALWAYS HAVE A BLACK BAND, WHICH ORIGINALLY COMMEMORATED THE DEATH OF QUEEN VICTORIA IN 1901

—⁂—

When construction of the Panama Canal got under way in the 1880s, the workforce took to wearing Panama hats as protection against the sun. This further cemented the misnomer and it has stuck ever since. Once Theodore Roosevelt was photographed wearing a Panama hat while being shown around the Canal in 1906, its universal appeal was assured. The weaving of Panama hats is a cottage industry carried out primarily in the districts of

Manabi and Azuay in Ecuador. Some of the more coarsely woven hats take only a few hours, while the finer hats (from the towns of Biblian and Montecristi) can take up to five months to weave. The greatest weavers work only by the light of the moon or when the sky is overcast. They dip their fingers in water, then split the fibre and plait ring after ring of palm into fabric. The most expensive Panamas are those with the tightest weave, clearly visible as a series of concentric rings emanating from the middle of the crown.

These concentric rings or *vueltas* indicate where new strands have been started in the weaving process. The number of vueltas determines the quality of the Panama. The cheaper hats, which may have taken a day or two to weave, will have roughly ten vueltas, while a superior quality Panama will contain as many as forty.

The best quality Panama hats sold in Britain always have a black band, which originally commemorated the death of Queen Victoria in 1901 and was never changed. Panama hats with a regimental or coloured band should be avoided, as should Panamas shaped like trilbies or other felt hats. The most stylish Panamas have a ridge along the top of the crown and can be folded into a tube for ease of transport.

Braces

When asked for his reaction to the outbreak of war in 1939, the actor Sir Ralph Richardson replied that he had gone straight to his tailor on Savile Row and purchased half a dozen pairs of Albert Thurston braces, in case they might be in short supply. So how did such a humble item as trouser suspension come to mean so much to chaps in the 1940s?

—⁘—

THE HIGH WAISTBANDS OF TROUSERS OF THE PERIOD MADE BRACES A NECESSITY

—⁘—

Stockings held up at the knee by a tied garter were common for both ladies and gentlemen from the middle Ages to the 18th century. Women's garters were hidden under their

skirts, but men's garters were often on display. Fashions evolved for tying one's garter ribbons in different ways – in *Twelfth Night*, Malvolio makes a fool of himself by wearing yellow stockings and cross garters.

By the late 18th century, young dandies and rakes wore the earliest braces, which kept their buckskin britches nice and tight, in keeping with the rather unambiguous male fashion of the day. Less privileged chaps wore trousers with a much looser fit, with braces known as "gallowses", which had an 'H' shape at the rear. This evolved into an 'X' back and in turn became the 'Y' shape still in use today.

Victorian braces were made of expensive materials like silk and satin and were patterned, usually with intricate embroidery depicting floral or animal motifs. The mass-marketed brace in cheaper fabrics like box-cloth and barrathea was invented by Albert Thurston in 1822. High waistbands, a legacy of the Regency era, ensured a more elegant line made by the trouser as it disappeared into the waistcoat.

Braces continued to be the most popular form of trouser support after the First World War, and it was only the adoption of the two-piece suit in the 1940s that led to their eventual demise. Braces were considered as underwear by gentlemen; it was therefore unseemly to allow them to be seen without the discreet covering of a waistcoat. Belts gradually replaced them, and the six buttons formerly attached to the outside of men's trousers moved quietly to the inside, and were eventually replaced by belt loops.

Gentlemen who wish to adopt a more traditional look, maintain smart trouser creases and, above all, not have to worry about post-prandial discomfort in the waist region, are strongly advised to return to braces.

Comte de Montesquiou

While Oscar Wilde (of whom too much has been written for us to delve into here) was heading for moral outrage in London, on the other side of the channel a Frenchman was hosting the sorts of literary salons at which Mr. Wilde would have been a welcome guest.

Comte Robert de Montesquiou-Fezensac was an eccentric poet, homosexual and saloniste. Close friends with Marcel Proust (who based his character Baron de Charlus on him) and the composer Gabriel Fauré, his salons at his Bois de Bologne mansion were the epicentre of fin-de-siècle bohemian Paris.

Montesquiou kept a menagerie of curious individuals at his home, in order to sustain the fantasy of living in a work of art. From Hata the Japanese gardener, who would shout at his master if requested to plant the wrong kind of tree, to Gabriel d'Yturri, Montesquiou's adoring Argentine factotum, whose duties included acquiring antiquities and curious and fighting duels on Montesquiou's behalf. Certain rooms in Montesquiou's home were themed to extremes: one room, called the snow chamber, had its temperature maintained to such a degree that fur coats were required to enter it.

Montesquiou himself displayed the unpredictable sartorial quirks of the true dandy. He once confounded his guests by appearing at a party dressed like a solicitor's clerk "to arouse a disappointed expectation of the ridiculous."

"HE ONCE APPEARED AT A PARTY DRESSED LIKE A SOLICITOR'S CLERK TO AROUSE A DISAPPOINTED EXPECTATION OF THE RIDICULOUS"

ANDRE GIDE

Fred Astaire

In his own words, Fred Astaire was just a "plain, ordinary guy from Omaha, Nebraska." He spent his whole life being self-conscious about his appearance, often comparing himself to Stan Laurel and adopting a variety of wigs when his hairline began to recede. An early screen test report, which Astaire himself often quoted when his success had been assured, read: "Can't act. Slightly bald. Also dances."

Fred Astaire went on to be described by Rudolph Nureyev as "the greatest American dancer in American history," and his place in the pantheon of dapper chaps is without question.

Astaire is widely credited with being the greatest influence on men's fashion of the 1930s. In *Top Hat* (1935) he first wore the ensemble that every man from London to Tokyo thereafter sought to emulate: soft-shouldered tweed sports coat, grey flannels, button-down collared shirt, striped tie, suede shoes and a voluminous pocket square. Astaire added his own peculiar details that no-one else could quite carry off, such as wearing a necktie as a belt and topping it all off with a straw boater. Astaire did away with the stuffy conventions that had preceded him, when men still wore the dark formal clothes of the Victorian era to work.

Astaire mixed the classic and the sporty, wearing white buck shoes with a plaid suit. The look defined a generation of Americans and has remained to this day, repackaged as the "preppy look" by designers like Ralph Lauren. Astaire was exhaustive in his quest for the right tailor for each element of his wardrobe, purchasing his shoes from Ireland, his shirts from America and his suits from England. He was a regular at Anderson and Sheppard, then on Savile Row, where a corner of the carpet would be lifted for him to ensure his new tail coat kept its shape in a dance move.

"CAN'T ACT. SLIGHTLY BALD. ALSO DANCES."

Astaire developed a look that was comfortable, contemporary, and, according to Irving Berlin, "simply reeks of class." But, like the man himself, that class was manifested in a very approachable and very American sense of the term.

8. DEMI MONDE

"A dead thing can go with the stream, but only
a living thing can go against it."
GK CHESTERTON

The Bohemian Chap

This fellow only just scrapes into the category of Chap due to a deep-seated, probably repressed urge to be a gentleman. His mis-spent youth devoted to rock 'n' roll music, foreign travel and marijuana cigarettes has left him ill-equipped to comfortably inhabit middle age, but at least a flat cap covers a receding hairline.

HABITAT

He still lives in a Housing Association basement flat in what was once a rough area of a city, but is now full of cappuccino bars and health food shops.

FEEDING

Nominally vegetarian, the Bohemian Chap has been known to sneak into a greasy spoon café and devour a bacon sandwich when his friends aren't looking.

MATING

An advocate of free love, he still goes "out on the pull" every weekend, though more and more frequently finds himself in awkward situations with friends of his grown-up daughters.

MIGRATION

Every year, the Bohemian Chap makes a pilgrimage to Glastonbury Music Festival, where he talks incessantly to youngsters about the days when "Hendrix blew the roof off", while they try to watch their favourite group.

Couples

Clip-on braces, absence of neckwear, see-through blouses, men marrying their daughters...this photograph can only have been sent from Australia.

"Attached is a photograph of myself and female companion, dressed for a fundraising dinner for the Memphis, Tennessee Roller Derby squad. While the invitation specified black-tie..." The writer, one Adam Remsen, felt the need to further explain his appalling outfit. I do not feel the need to print it here. The expression on his companion's face (who dresses remarkably well, under the circumstances) says it all.

"**M**yself and my fine companion Camboli recently attended a very fine tea party hosted by some lovely fellows at Avalon Television," wrote Brian Kneedeep.

Really? No wonder there is so much drivel on television these days.

"**A**ttached is a photo of the delectable Mrs Montellier and I," writes Clive Montellier, "indulging ourselves with afternoon tea in the midst of a weekend of Noel Coward-related frolics. If only the real world were not just across the sands..."

Sir, the real world is closer than you think. It's on your shirt in the form of a breast pocket – which no half-decent shirt should possess. I am surprised your good lady has not walked away in disgust, for you are insulting her by not wearing a hat nor a jacket while out-of-doors and in her company.

Motoring Chaps

It is rare indeed to find no fault whatsoever in a chap's raiment, despite careful scrutiny from top to tail. But before one can make a unanimous declaration of chapdom, one must of course read the accompanying letter to the photograph, in case there is anything there to cause reasonable doubt: "I wondered if the attached photograph may be of some interest to you?," wrote Phil Squires. "Sadly the 4.5 Litre Bentley is not mine" Ah – there you go.

"This photograph was taken," writes Miss Sarah Johnson, "whilst waiting to pick up friends for a day-trip. The car is a 1957 Wolseley 15/50 of which I am the lucky owner."

Madam, why can't all ladies be like you? Not only is your motor vehicle exemplary, but we can heap only praise on your intelligently assembled outfit and expertly applied maquillage.

Yes, everything seems to be in order here...and yet...it's all just a little too neat and perfect. Go on man, hurl her into the back seat of the Mercedes and crumple your lapels a bit...put some life into that stiff suit!

Motoring Chaps

The trouble with sending one's offspring to Oxford is that they all end up trying to emulate the characters in *Brideshead Revisited*. These two, however, have barely managed to conjure up a very low-budget puppet version of *The Wind in the Willows*.

The use of a sports car as a shooting stick is rather novel, though one wonders whether the suspension of a 1964 MGB is adequate to support the extra weight. A nice choice of vehicle though, being the car of choice for a cad and his bird in the 1960s – although the bird was usually alive.

This red convertible will have no trouble supporting "Johnny's" limp frame, but is he using it merely to distract us from his rather lacklustre pantaloons, his ill-fitting smoking jacket and his lank hair? And what is his motor vehicle doing in the living room anyway?

Bohemian Chaps

How does one know that this fellow is of the bohemian persuasion? Well, despite an impressive lip weasel, he's deliberately left a bit of hair on his chin to show that he's a rebel; he is wearing some sort of lapel badge to display his humorous side, and his spectacles are of the variety worn by people who spend a lot of time loafing about in art galleries. He's also drinking Continental lager, out-of-doors – not the habit of a true gentleman.

If proof were required, which it isn't, that no attempts should ever be made to unite the dictates of gentlemen's dress with those of haute-couture fashion, then this is it.

When the gentlemen of the East India Company first explored the uncharted lands of the Orient, and returned laden with fine silks and satins, printed with exotic designs that spoke of illicit boudoirs and foppish lotus eaters, these were not the customers they had in mind.

What these Bohemians do, in order to confound expectation, is to lure you in with the sense that all is right with their wardrobe and that one is among fellow chaps – and then floor you with some dreadful faux-pas, calculated to shock and outrage you. In this fellow's case, it is allowing too many links of his watch chain to hang from the fob.

Billy Childish

Deep in the heart of northern Kent there exists a rather insalubrious place called Chatham. A former bustling port, little of note occurs there apart from the odd street fight between lovers.

However, occasionally the rooftops of Chatham shudder with a strange, ancient sound: that of an electric guitar being played through a valve amplifier. The Men of Kent prick up their ears and say, in their strange dialect: "That Billy Childish is releasing a new album."

Mr. Childish is known as much for the variety of his oeuvre – he paints, plays music, writes poetry and is a keen hill walker – as his prodigious output. He has released over 100 albums of beat music, painted some 2000 paintings and published 40 volumes of poetry. Billy's wardrobe favours the working man's clothes of the late Victorian era to the 1940s; he is happier in a knotted bandana than a four-in-hand, and prefers to wear hob nailed boots rather than brogues. This makes for a very distinctive look, catered for by clothing companies such as Old Town and the Vintage Shirt Company (see Directory).

Billy's strong opinions are as rooted in traditional craftsmanship as his clothing; he is a firm believer in the materialism and aesthetics of the Victorians, compared to the lack of interest in materials and disposability of today's manufacturers. "If you gave a Victorian a Nike running shoe," he says, "he might say, 'ok, it's light, practical – where can I get it resoled?' When you told him that you just throw them away, he'd think you were nuts!"

"I dress more like my dad's gardener than like my dad. I prefer to have my clothes made by underpaid craftsmen in England than underpaid children abroad."

"I DRESS MORE LIKE MY DAD'S GARDENER

THAN LIKE MY DAD"

The Bowler Hat

In 1850 **William Coke** went to St James's hatters Lock & Co. with a conundrum. His gamekeepers were constantly losing or damaging their top hats while out riding around the estate. Mr. Coke asked whether Lock could fashion a lower hat with a rounder crown, but with the resilience of a topper.

A prototype of Mr. Coke's design was duly constructed from layers of muslin stiffened with shellac, and he was invited to come and view it. The first thing he did was take the hat outside and jump up and down on it on the pavement. He declared the hat a success, and, in accordance with Lock & Co.'s tradition, it was christened the 'Coke' in his honour. Once the Coke caught on, other versions appeared, made by hatters Bowler Bros, and it soon came to be known as a bowler, though at Lock & Co. it continues to be known as a Coke. The Americans call it a 'Derby', after the race meetings at which it was once worn.

Having started life in the country, the Coke migrated to the city where, by the Edwardian era, it had replaced the top hat among barristers, stockbrokers and civil servants, and it remained firmly clamped upon their heads until the 1980s. In such environs, the Coke has now been replaced by either no

—w—

IT IS DIFFICULT TO THINK OF
A MORE QUINTESSENTIALLY
ENGLISH SIGHT THAN HUNDREDS
OF MEN IN IDENTICAL BLACK
SUITS, MARCHING IN UNISON,
WEARING BOWLER HATS AND
BEARING FURLED UMBRELLAS

—w—

hat at all, or the sort of hat designed to shade the eyes of an American Rounders player. The latter deserves nothing less than the treatment meted out by Mr. Lock on his prototype Coke in 1850.

Today the Coke is still the civilian hat of guard's officers, as displayed every year in the Combined Cavalry Old Comrades Association parade in Hyde Park. It is difficult to think of a more quintessentially English sight than hundreds of men in identical black suits, marching in unison, wearing bowler hats and bearing furled umbrellas.

Tommy Nutter

Tommy Nutter is still a legend on Savile Row, fondly remembered as one of the great innovators of the trade, responsible for injecting a much-needed boost into British bespoke tailoring during its slump at the tail end of the swinging sixties.

In 1969 he opened House of Nutter at 35, Savile Row, with financial help from Cilla Black and Peter Brown of Apple Records. House of Nutter quickly established a reputation for flashy, exciting styles with the contemporary flair of Carnaby Street combined with high-quality tailoring. "Everybody was wearing a narrow suit at the end of the 1960s," said Nutter, "so I just went wild with the lapels and cut them as wide as you possibly could – enormous – and it was terribly flared at the jacket." Soon the noted hipsters of the decade were queuing up to be suited by Nutter. Mick and Bianca Jagger were married in matching Nutter white trouser suits in 1971; three Beatles wore Nutter suits on the cover of Abbey Road (George Harrison rebelled by wearing jeans}; and David Bowie wore a powder-blue Nutter suit for the cover of his long-player Pinups.

Nutter didn't restrict himself to clothing pop stars. He could also make traditional tweed suits and lounge suits for aristocrats, who certainly didn't want enormous lapels and padded shoulders. He continued trading on the Row, under various different shop names, until his death in 1992.

The man who looked best in Tommy Nutter's suits was Tommy Nutter. He had the verve and natural flamboyance to get away with clashing tweeds, huge bow ties and extremely pinched waists. In 1971 he was elected to the Best-Dressed List in the United States, along with the Earl of Snowdon and Hardy Amies. American Menswear magazine described him as 'tradition spiced with daring'.

Nutter was much loved on the Row and beyond by a wide circle of cultured friends, who revered his gentle, self-deprecating personality and his witty remarks, always ending with the expression "But who am I to talk?" He delighted in writing to the serious newspapers on topics as wide ranging as the correct buttoning of the suit on a statue of John F. Kennedy to the scarcity of deckchairs in Green Park.

9. FIGHTING SPIRIT

"He only went into the Army to put his
moustache to good purpose."
ALAN BENNETT

The Military Chap

In a sense all chaps are military chaps, though all members of the armed forces are not necessarily chaps. A squaddie would expect to receive a comfort box full of pornography and crisps, while an officer chap would rather have one filled with Gentlemen's Relish and water biscuits. Only officers have chap aspirations, and their world of mess rooms, rigid dress codes and arcane hierarchies bring them closer in spirit to the Old World than the rest of us.

HABITAT

Wherever the latest theatre of war happens to be, the military chap will take his snuff, his gaiters and his monocle with him.

FEEDING

He will either stuff his face and get horribly plastered during an eight-course regimental dinner, or survive on a tin of lard for a week during battle, without once complaining.

MATING

Twice a year while on annual leave, and thrice at Christmas if the enemy isn't playing up.

MIGRATION

The military chap is in a permanent state of migration, though he is very good at turning a corner of a foreign field into England.

Military Chaps

It must be fun being in the RAF: the camaraderie, the airborne thrills, the opportunity to sport exuberant facial hair and look the bees knees in uniform.
 This poor fellow wouldn't stand a chance.

If one were in a battalion of stormtroopers, one would be quaking in one's jackboots at the sight of Tommy and Phil of the Tommy Atkins Society. With laughter.

A ha. A real soldier. A real gun. A real magazine.

But surreal trousers and a shirt that hasn't been ironed properly. Weather looks nice though. Where are you, Mallorca?

A t first I took this to be a photograph of some plastic dummies in a military museum, but upon closer inspection it turned out to be nothing more than some bits of old rubbish piled up in a corner.

Sporting Chaps

'David' managed to find himself a boating blazer two sizes too small for him, without a breast pocket on which to place the badge. He then decided to wear it anyway, with a club tie in different colours. Then, rather than go boating, he went off to play tennis.

Michael Simm opens his missive by complaining about the state of dress on today's golf courses. Yet he submits this photograph. Jimmy Tarbuck circa 1974 would have displayed more panache than this silly man, who is so focused on mocking a much-maligned (and therefore beyond mockery) genre that there is nothing left of him for anyone to see. He is therefore neither a Chap, nor even a man.

"With the approach of summer," writes Mr A. Kerensky, FRSA, "I wonder if you can offer some advice with headwear. How do I pick a good Panama, for example?"

Well, since you ask: Panamas should in some way complement what one is wearing, so in your case I would try and find one with a comedy flower print on it, two sizes too large, and which squirts water out of the crown when you press the brim.

Albion

Albion has already taken a mysterious pseudonym redolent of ancient England, yet he goes one further, and takes a second nom-de-plume: The Geovictwardian.

Albion's aesthetic is a complex one which operates on many levels: he is deeply interested in paganism with special reference to Earth Mysteries; yet his waistcoats belie a similarly profound attachment to English tailoring of the Edwardian period. His interest in swordsmanship, archery and Bartitsu (the gentlemanly martial art devised by Edward Barton-Wright in the 1890s) confirm his enthusiasm for the arts of the Victorian gentleman.

In what capacity does the Geovictwardian operate? He simply exists, dressed immaculately, floating around the various sacred areas of these fair isles, such as Cerne Abbas, Lindisfarne and Jermyn Street, to investigate, absorb and understand his findings there. "If contemporary society is examined," says Albion, "many Geovictwardians are already all around us, behaving with good manners, dressing well and adopting wholesome habits and modes of living. These are not effete parvenus or aristocrats; these are certain types of people who wish to be classless and stylish, but with substance."

"THERE IS NO POINT IN HAVING

A BEAUTIFUL WELL-MADE SUIT UNLESS YOU

HAVE A REAL MAN TO PUT IN IT"

The Pith Helmet

The pith helmet, also known as the sola topi (but never the solar topee) evolved during Britain's Empire-enlarging sprint across tropical lands. Pale, wan English chaps simply didn't tolerate the relentless sun, particularly in India, where an indigenous plant known as the sola provided the solution. The pith of the sola was fashioned by Indian milliners into a light, strong and all-covering hat suitable for the effete Englishman. Early pith helmets featured a peak at the front and rear, with white cloth completely covering the hat and a pair of small holes for ventilation.

When Henry Stanley decided to embark on his quest to find David Livingstone in 1871, his first port of call was Gieves of Savile Row, where he ordered a pith helmet. No other form of headwear would have made sense on a 700-mile trek through challenging conditions. Another great traveller of the day, Mary Kingsley, who escaped her native Islington and headed for Angola and Luanda, wore a white pith helmet held in place with a length of fine fabric, which detail came to be known as a puggaree.

The ultimate accolade for the pith helmet came when the British army adopted it in 1870. However, the bright

white colour proved a dangerous giveaway in battle, and infantrymen, eager to prolong their duty for as long as possible, began to dye their topis with a mixture of tea, ground coffee beans and cattle dung. In 1881, Viscount Cardwell introduced the Cardwell system, which adorned pith helmets with each county's own individually named regiment. Civilian pith helmets were of similar dimensions to their military cousins, though lacking the badges, regimental star plates and brass spikes representing the various brigades.

The Royal Marines still wear white "Wolseley pattern" pith helmets as part of their Number Ones. They are ornamented with a brass ball ornament on top, a helmet plate and chin chain. Foreign regiments with enough flair to continue wearing pith helmets include the Tongan Royal Guard, the Compagnie des Carabiniers du Prince du Monaco and the Sri Lankan Police.

The practice of British diplomats in tropical postings wearing sola topis as part of their ceremonial white uniforms died out in the 1980s. The last time any of them were seen in pith helmets was during the ceremonies marking the end of British rule in Hong Kong in 1997.

The Blazer

When Queen Victoria arranged a visit to the frigate HMS Blazer in 1837, the Captain took one look at his crew and thought, "What an absolute shower!" He promptly asked the regimental tailor (probably Gieves & Hawkes) to run up some smart coats for the crew to wear during the royal visit. Their starting point were the heavy double-breasted blue reefer coats with brass buttons worn by midshipmen on deck.

What Queen Victoria was presented with was an orderly crew all dressed in short navy blue serge coats with brass buttons bearing the naval crest. She liked what she saw, and before long all crew members were issued with blazers.

This evolved into the blazer we know today, with a few modifications. The naval blazers were double-breasted, whereas modern blazers can be single-breasted as well. Naval blazers had flap pockets, while club or school blazers usually have patch side pockets, and always a patch breast pocket, so the relevant badge can be attached. Though the brass buttons remain, they needn't carry any insignia and are often plain flat brass.

But of more interest to Chaps is the club blazer, an entirely different species of coat. These originated with the oarsmen of the Lady Margaret Boat Club of Cambridge in the early 20th century, who wore scarlet jackets that were often described as being "ablaze". They evolved into the boating blazer, either in a single colour or with vertical stripes in club or college colours, with a badge on the breast pocket. They are worn with white or cream flannels and a straw boater, whereas navy blazers are usually worn with grey slacks, a cravat and a lascivious grin, with perhaps the addition of a monocle for the truly deranged.

—⁓—

SCARLET JACKETS WERE OFTEN DESCRIBED AS BEING "ABLAZE"

—⁓—

David Niven

There was nothing remarkable about David Niven's dress, but coupled with his immense charm, good looks and way with the ladies, it all added up to an archetype of the English officer class that the American movie industry was more than happy to adopt.

Niven himself, in his autobiography *The Moon's a Balloon*, claimed to have arrived in Hollywood via a steamer that he had boarded during a party on a yacht the previous night, then fallen asleep in. His entrance to breakfast in a crumpled dinner jacket paints a lovely image, even though probably embellished somewhat by the skilled raconteur. Whether true or not, Niven was never kicked out of anywhere, least of all Hollywood, and only left a glittering movie career briefly, to serve his country as a commando in the Second World War.

NIVEN DEVELOPED A SKILL FOR CONSOLING THE LONELY WIVES OF NAVAL OFFICERS ON LONG STINTS AT SEA

Having been through Stowe School and Sandhurst, Niven had already accumulated the wardrobe of the English sporting gentleman: grey flannels for weekdays, navy suits for Sundays, cricket whites and cable knit jumpers, as well as the formal wardrobe that was to accompany him on his flights of the imagination. Sandhurst had also introduced him to Savile Row, where he joined the client list at Watson, Fagerstrom & Hughes, Benson Perry & Whitly and the original Hawes & Curtis, all of whom have ceased to exist in their original form. Dispatched to Malta, Niven learned polo, picked up a wardrobe of well-tailored tropicals and developed a skill for consoling the lonely wives of naval officers on long stints at sea.

Wherever he went, Niven was always impeccably dressed and ready with a *bon mot*. During a speech at the Oscars, clad in a bottle-green smoking jacket and black tie, he calmly dealt with a streakier rushing on stage as he presented an academy award by saying, "The only way that man will ever get a laugh is by stripping off and showing his shortcomings."

Anthony Eden

It is extremely rare for politicians to display any flamboyance in their dress, and even rarer for British prime ministers. Anthony Eden is the exception. The poster boy of post-war politics, he sent teenage girls into a frenzy wherever he travelled, leading American newspapers to gush about "his classic features, his long dark eyelashes, his limpid eyes, his clear skin, his wavy hair, his charm and magnetism".

BERTRAND RUSSELL CLAIMED THAT EDEN WAS NOT A GENTLEMAN BECAUSE HE DRESSED TOO WELL

Sartorially he was not without innovation, or at least unafraid to part with convention. He wore linen waistcoats with lounge suits and Astrakhan-collared coats. His trademark Homburg became such an international icon that it soon earned the new moniker of an "Anthony Eden". One American hat shop, on the eve of a visit by the PM to the town, put up a sign reading "Welcome to Anthony Eden".

Like all men fastidious about their dress, Eden had to put up with a lot of ribbing and snide comments regarding his clothes (which he probably enjoyed, as they secured his position as an icon). Malcolm Muggeridge described him thus: "An elegant appearance and an earnest disposition equipped him for dazzling advancement. An astrakhan collar became him. What came to be known as an Anthony Eden hat grew on heads like his." W.F. Deedes, who had once commented unfavourably on the colour of Eden's socks, remarked that, in the modern vernacular, Eden was a "smoothie". Bertrand Russell went even further, claiming that Eden was not a gentleman because he dressed too well.

Eden's Homburg became his trademark and the butt of cartoonists who criticised his handling of the Suez crisis. But in truth Eden was defiantly modernist in his hat wearing, and by the 1950s often appeared in public wearing no hat at all. Such was the power of his image that everybody saw a Homburg on his head even when he wasn't wearing one. Not quite the Emperor's new clothes, but nevertheless a persuasive bit of iconography.

NEW HORIZONS

"The only time my education was interrupted
was when I was at school."
GEORGE BERNARD SHAW

Hip Chap

This new species has only recently been discovered, when a stray specimen hopped into the garden of Dr. Aloysius Membrane, who happened to be compiling an exhaustive volume on the Chappist genus. Having satisfied himself that it was not some mutant creature, perhaps created as a joke by the North Koreans, Dr. Membrane immediately killed it and added it to his collection.

HABITAT

The extremely fashionable quarters of major cities such as London and Tokyo.

FEEDING

The hip chap subsists almost entirely on Earl Grey tea and Brandy Snaps, which he always insists on ordering from outlets highly unlikely to serve them, such as Starbucks.

MATING

Hip chaps never mate, as they are far too preoccupied with deciding whether Paisley will be fashionable that day or the next.

MIGRATION

The hip chap makes regular trips to the fashion centres of the world, purely to ensure that his outfits have absolutely nothing to do with what is happening on the catwalks of Milan or Paris.

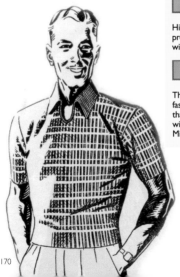

Hiroki

Hiroki Ohashi from Tokyo commenced his voluminous correspondence with *The Chap* with this rather unpromising photograph showing an unflattering combination of hairy overcoat and bad teeth. But then the flood of missives began, and Mr. Ohashi's true colours emerged...

Hiroki then upped his game by showing that he was making frequent visits to menswear outlets and taking a serious look at coat linings. I felt that he deliberately chose the duffle to show that we were all prepared to move on from any lingering frostiness that had existed between the Imperial Japanese Navy and the Royal Navy after the Second World War.

By this stage, Hiroki was beginning to show genuine Chappist potential, having progressed to wearing a tie. He was also becoming more comfortable about revealing the humility of his living accommodation. However, there was clearly still a great deal of work of to be done on his wardrobe, particularly regarding his choice of footwear.

"Sir," wrote Hiroki in his most spirited letter to *The Chap*, "I found a pair of fantastic shoes. That's made in Japan of 1980s, not in 20s. Looks so delicious also!" By this stage I realised that Mr. Ohashi had entirely understood the tenets of our credo, and that he needed no further guidance from me.

Youth Cult Chaps

'Laird' Noel James Kelly sent a rather tiresome missive with his picture, which purported to make amusing comments about the aristocracy being forced to travel on public transport. Yet there is nothing amusing about wearing a tie under one's shirt, exposing chest hair, not shaving and wearing welder's goggles. There appears to be no ice or lemon in the G&T either. Laird indeed!

Tragedy has clearly struck this hapless pair of proto-Chaps. They must have been set upon by a brigand of ruffians, for one has had his jacket, hat and socks stolen, and his trousers replaced with those of a teenage girl. The other unfortunate fellow was obviously stripped entirely, and was then dressed in a way designed to utterly humiliate him in front of his friends.

There is nothing wrong with mods: they like well-cut suits, barbiturates and swaggering about, but it is a youth cult best left behind after reaching the age of 20. Once one is beginning to say goodbye to one's hair, flat stomach and ability to judge the right colour for a suit fabric, then it is time to move on, perhaps to being a rocker. They tend to age more majestically, or at least die while still in their prime.

Youth Cult Chaps

This young shaver is heading in the right direction, yet still has a long way to go. His cape is far too small for him and he has tied his scarf as a cravat. After that it just gets worse: the list beginning with the gap betwixt trouser and waistcoat and going on far too long to conclude here. On the positive side, he has remembered to unfasten one of his waistcoat buttons – but the wrong one.

This fellow has clearly got "Dinner Jacket" and "Disc Jockey" mixed up, for he is pursuing the latter without wearing the former. Quite what he is doing wearing a hat indoors is anyone's guess, but at least it sits comfortably upon his ear-muffs.

Now this is more like it! If one really must be young, then why not do so in as bold a manner as possible, while adhering to the gentlemanly credo? Why not set out to stop traffic, rather than simply achieve a nod of approval from some old duffer, or, worse still, the approbation of one's parents?

Mr B The Gentleman Rhymer

Popular music is not a field of endeavour calculated to distract a gentleman from his daily business, and the sub-genre known as "hip-hop" is more likely to have him calling the Noise Abatement Society than tapping his toes. However, a sprightly cove calling himself Mr. B has decided to turn his fascination with this form of American "gangsta" music into a palatable form for those with more refined manners.

Mr. B the Gentleman Rhymer follows his job description to the letter, in that he creates amusing rhyming couplets in a gentlemanly idiom, to a backbeat that can only be described as Public Enemy crossed with George Formby. His subject matter includes watching cricket at the Oval, wearing a "Sherry Monocle" and the joys of smoking crack cocaine. The targets of his gentle satirical stabs range from Timothy Westwood's comically inverted snobbery to the government's ban on smoking in *Let me Smoke My Pipe*: "I'll abide by the rules of your watering holes/But I won't stand in the rain with a pack of bloody proles."

Mr. B, however, is no jonathan-come-lately. He is a veteran, albeit with a now much improved wardrobe, of the British hip-hop scene, with a sound grasp of the technical boffinery required to scratch, sample, mix and generally cobble together what young people like to dance the "twist" to these days.

"WE'VE UPPED OUR STANDARDS,

NOW UP YOURS TOO"

The Fair Isle Sweater

Fair Isle is Britain's most remote inhabited island. Situated midway between the Shetlands and the Orkneys, it is a tiny island with a population of 70 people, 1,000 sheep and 150,000 seabirds. Fair Isle has long held prime position on the Chap's world map by producing a unique traditional knitting style. The sweaters, usually sleeveless, feature geometric rows of distinctive knitted shapes, some influenced by the iconography of the island, such as anchors, rams' horns, ferns and flowers. It is not known what gave rise to this style – possible influences range from a wrecked Spanish Armada ship in 1588, to religious iconography, or the knitwear sported by passing Baltic fishermen. The colours originally came from the limited natural palette within sheep's wool – white, grey, black, brown, red, ochre. Then natural plant dyes were added, such as lichen and amphibious bistort – an attractive floating pond plant with cylindrical spikes of delicate pink flowers.

Unlike Harris Tweed, the term "Fair Isle" is not a registered trademark. "Fair Isle" has become a generic term for any patterned sweater. The only exceptions are garments bearing the term "made in Fair Isle", which cannot be made anywhere else. The only place you can buy a new genuine Fair Isle sweater is at one of the knitters' houses or by mail order. Occasionally, cruise ships pass by, and the knitters put on a small display in the village hall. Even then, production is minute and defines the term cottage industry. There are just four part-time knitters working on hand frames, producing about 100 sweaters a year.

Despite the Duke of Windsor popularising Fair Isle sweaters in the 1920s, they were never mass-produced, though recently many fashion houses have made their own machine-knitted versions. It is not uncommon to find the genuine hand-knitted article in vintage clothing stores. They are best worn with Harris Tweed plus fours and a heavy tweed jacket. Like most gentlemen's clothing in the post-Edward VIII universe, Fair Isle sweaters are far too good for the golf course.

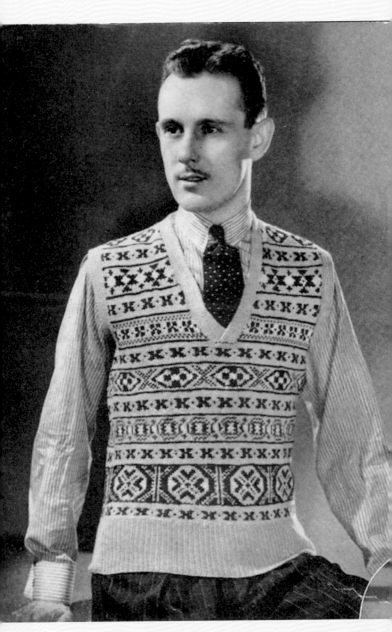

Pyjamas

Though it has its roots in the Persian word for "leg covering", the word pyjama entered into English via the Hindi word "paijama". When colonials began returning to Britain from the East in the mid 19th century, among their many souvenirs were loose, drawstring trousers worn by Sikh gentlemen, in which they had spent many a sultry afternoon lounging about under a fan in the Punjab. In Britain's colder climate, these paijamas lent themselves perfectly to nightwear.

Pyjamas gained an anglicised spelling and gradually replaced the traditional night-shirt for gentlemen to sleep in. By the 1930s they were practically a fashion item, having gained sartorial flourishes borrowed liberally from day wear, such as pockets, collars and turn-back cuffs. Some men even wore them at home; with the addition of

a silk dressing gown, pyjamas became the ideal outfit for literary types to affect the air of a weary aesthete. They also prevented time being wasted on the mundane task of getting ready for bed.

The cut of men's pyjamas has always followed contemporary fashions. In the 1930s they were cut wide in the leg all the way down and some had turnups. By the 1960s they were much narrower in the leg, which then flared out again in the 1970s before settling on a widish, baggy cut today which harks back to the 1930s again. Pyjamas are traditionally

made from warm, rough fabrics such as cotton twill, Wynciette and flannelette.

In these days of many of us working from home, a comfortable yet durable pair of pyjamas is essential, as the particularly fastidious worker may forget to get dressed in the morning before addressing the day's tasks. When his friends turn up for cocktails at 5pm, and he is still wearing his cotton pyjamas and silk dressing gown, he will not feel in the slightest bit underdressed.

Edward VIII

Few individuals have been as important in 20th century sartorial history as the Duke of Windsor. He was almost solely responsible for putting a splash of colour into gentlemen's wardrobes, after the dark, formal tones of the Edwardian period. Edward VIII was the first man to make it acceptable for men to be as colourful as their female counterparts.

The Duke's look became so iconic and influential that we now think of it as the look of the age. Plus fours in a ginger Harris Tweed, with slanted pockets, worn with harlequin socks and a Fair Isle sweater? Nobody had ever dressed like that on the golf course before the Duke of Windsor, and soon everyone from the local bank manager to Crown Prince Hirohito of Japan was doing the same.

> HE WAS ALMOST SOLELY RESPONSIBLE FOR PUTTING A SPLASH OF COLOUR INTO GENTLEMEN'S WARDROBES

Unlike his rather portly grandfather, Edward VIII was blessed with a trim, angular frame that made the job of his numerous tailors uncomplicated. Neither did his shape change significantly over the years, meaning that he was able to fit into suits made for him decades earlier. The Duke was obsessed with clothes and, rather than make endlessly complicated travel arrangements with them, he kept a full wardrobe at his regular destinations throughout the world. He constantly carried with him a series of small boxes containing cloth samples, which he would whip out in Paris, Milan or New York to compare the colours of what he was buying with what he already owned.

Edward favoured Savile Row tailor Frederick Scholte for his jackets, but usually had his trousers made at the American company of Forster & Sons. His frequent visits to Scholte were recorded in his sartorial autobiography *Windsor Revisited*. On one occasion, Edward was greatly amused to see his equerry Fruity Metcalfe being turned away by Scholte for requesting wider shoulders and a narrower waist on a coat.

TAILORS

NORTON & SONS
One of the oldest houses on Savile Row, Norton & Sons combines centuries-old tradition with a few contemporary touches.
Nortonandsons.co.uk
16 Savile Row, London, W1S 3PL
020 7437 0829

JAMES PERSONAL TAILOR & SON
Bespoke tailor of 40 years standing offering traditional and contemporary styles
www.jamespersonaltailor.co.uk
52 Cross Street
Manchester
M2 7AR
0161 8327678

JASPER LITTMAN
Bespoke and semi bespoke suits measured, fitted and delivered by visiting tailors to locations in the South East. Prices range from £699-£799.
Jasperlittman.co.uk
9 Savile Row, London, W1S 3PF
08456 121 220

PETER SMITHARD
A fully bespoke suit for only £250-£700. Refreshingly there is no web site, so telephone for an appointment
134 Domestic Street, Leeds, LS11 9SG
0113 243 3880

CAD AND THE DANDY
Made-to-measure and bespoke tailors with travelling tailor to visit any office in Central London.
Cadandthedandy.co.uk
4 Castle Court, The City, London, EC3V 9DL
020 7283 1975

A SUIT THAT FITS
This (ridiculously named) company offers bespoke tailoring at bargain prices by taking your measurements in the UK then farming out the tailoring to Nepal. Prices around £250 for a two-piece suit (that fits).
Asuitthatfits.com
38 Glasshouse Street, London, W1B 5DL
0203 0067999

BOOKSTER
Made-to-order service with a price tag in the region of £450 for a 3-piece tweed suit.
Tweed-jacket.com
The Granary, Hildersley Farm. Hildersley, Ross on Wye, Herefordshire, HR9 7NW
01989 562212

SPENCERS TROUSERS
Made to measure trousers individually cut and tailored in their West Yorkshire workrooms, in a huge range of pure new wool tweeds and over 400 authentic tartans.
www.spencers-trousers.com
01422 833020

COUNTRY OUTFITTERS

BARBOUR
For all your waxed coats and winter woollens.
www.barbour.com for a full list of branches
123 Sydney Street, King's Road, Chelsea, Central London, SW3 6NR
020 73525346

CORDINGS
The one-stop shop for tweeds, corduroys and moleskins in a kaleidoscope of colours.
www.cordings.co.uk
London, W1J 0LA
0207 734 0830

WHIPPERLEYS
On-line store for country, military and adventure wear, from pith helmets to flying goggles.
Whipperleys.co.uk

FORMAL OUTFITTERS

BUDD SHIRTMAKERS LTD
One of only two UK outlets that sell boiled-front formal shirts
1 Piccadilly Arcade,
www.londontown.com
St James's, London, SW1Y 6NH
020 7493 0139

DARCY CLOTHING LTD
2, Mount Place Lewes BN7 1YH
www.darcyclothing.com
01273 477699
The other vendor of quality formal shirts, which also sells vintage-style informal wear (see also under shirtmakers).

CLERMONT DIRECT
A bit of a bin-end for formal wear, nevertheless useful for the odd bow tie or collar stud needed in a rush
ClermontDirect.com

GENTS OUTFITTERS

LIPMAN & SONS
Small, friendly family company offering suits, separates and accessories to buy or hire for any occasion
www.lipmanandsons.co.uk
22 Charing Cross Road, London WC2
020 7240 2310

OLD TOWN
Vendor of high-quality suits, jackets and trousers made from authentic 1930s patterns, all made in their charming factory in Norfolk
www.old-town.co.uk
49 Bull Street, Holt, Norfolk NR25 6HP
01263 710001

SHIRTMAKERS

CHARLES TYRWHITT
www.ctshirt.co.uk
92 Jermyn Street, London, SW1Y 6JB
020 7839 6060

HARVIE & HUDSON
The Jermyn Street store retains its bespoke department while the website offers made-to-measure shirts with detachable stiff collars and neck bands.
www.harvieandhudeson.com
96/97 Jermyn Street, London, SW1 6JE
0207 839 3578

HILDITCH & KEY
One of the Old Guard of St James's and still turning out decent collars and patterns.
Hilditchandkey.co.uk
37 Jermyn Street, London, SW1 6DT
020 7734 4707

NEW & LINGWOOD
Shirtmakers to the pupils of Eton School, among others.
Newandlingwood.com
53 Jermyn Street, London, SW1Y 6LX
020 7493-9621

STEPHAN HAROUTUNIAN SHIRTS LTD
Bespoke shirts at prices a long way from Jermyn Street, by a genial Cypriot whose business dates back to the 1950s.
Stephanshirts.co.uk
95 Moore Park Road, Fulham, London, SW6 2DA
020 7731 5008

TURNBULL & ASSER
Distinctive made-to-measure and ready-made service since 1885, which prides itself on customer relations.
Turnbullandasser.com
71/72 Jermyn Street, London, SW1Y 6PF
0207 808 3001

DARCY CLOTHING LTD
The only British supplier of 1930s-style spearpoint collared shirts, in a beautiful array of patterns as well as plain white. They also specialise in formal shirtings and separate stiff collars.
2, Mount Place Lewes BN7 1YH
www.darcyclothing.com
01273 477699

HATTERS

BATES HATS
Bates-hats.co.uk
Temporarily located at 73, Jermyn Street, London, SW1Y 6JD
020 7734 2722

BRENT BLACK
Every style of panama under one roof, of this established American company.
Brentblack.com
(808) 262-2892

CHRISTYS
In actual fact a headwear wholesaler,
but the entire range is available through
Hornets Hats in Kensington
www.hornetshats.co.uk
Christys-hats.com
Christys' & Company Limited, Unit
7, Witan Park, Station Lane, Avenue 2,
Witney, Oxon, OX28 4FH
01993 770736

CLASSIC HATS
Gentleman's hat, cap and accessory
emporium based in the achingly
fashionable area of Columbia Road in
London's East End and Covent Garden.
www.classic-hats.com
128 Columbia Rd, London, E2 7RG
23 New Row, Covent Garden, London,
WC2N 4LA.
020 7240 4240

JAMES LOCK & CO
Founded in 1676, James Lock & Co. is the
oldest family-owned hat shop in the world,
whose customers have included Lord
Byron and Oscar Wilde.
Lockhatters.co.uk
6 St. James's Street, London, SW1A 1EF
020 7930 8874

PACHACUTI
The hat department of this fair trade
company offers a diverse range of
authentic Ecuadorian Panamas shipped
directly from where they are made.
Panamas.co.uk
19 Dig Street, Ashbourne, Derbyshire,
DE6 1GF
01335 300 003

T. SNOOK
Charming little shop in a charming market
town crammed to the rafters with titfers
of every description, including a few
exclusive to Snook.
Snooksthehatters.co.uk
32 West Street, Bridport, Dorset, DT6
3QP
01308 458224

JW MYERS
Maker of flat caps for 110 years exporting
to 22 countries, bought by Kangol in the
early 21st century.
Saville Works, Shafton Lane, Leeds, West
Yorkshire, LS11 9QZ
0843 273 9278

VINTAGE CLOTHING

BEYOND RETRO
A vintage clothing superstore, where
one may lose oneself in aisle upon aisle
of lovingly arranged men's and women's
clothing from the 1940s to the 1980s.
Beyondretro.com
110-112 Cheshire Street, London E2 6EJ
020 7613 3636
42 Vine Street
Brighton BN1 4AG
+44 (0)1273 671 937

BIRDS DRESS AGENCY
The clothes in this out-of-the way shop
are as musty and redolent of a more
agreeable era as one would wish.
251-253 Malpas Road, London SE4
Tel 020 8692 0333

BLACKOUT II
A gem of a shop stocking men's and ladies'
vintage clobber from the 1940 upwards.
A generous selection of dinner suits,
morning coats and overcoats.
Blackout2.com
Blackout II, 51 Endell Street, Covent
Garden, London, WC2H 9AJ
020 7240 5006

CLASSIC CHAPS
This shop, like the clothes, recalls an era
when going shopping meant being served
by nice chaps behind the counter, tape
measure at the ready.
Classicchaps.co.uk
Cinq Ports Street, Rye, Sussex, TN31 7NA.
07918 664512

ECHOES
One of Britain's best and most remote
vintage clothing outlets, with men's and
womenswear from the 1900s to the
1950s.
Echovintage.com
650a Halifax Road, Eastwood, Todmorden,
West Yorkshire, OL14 6DW.
01706 817505.

FROCK ME! VINTAGE FAIRS
Bi-monthly vintage fairs held in London
and Brighton, specialising in clothing from
the 18th century upwards. The prices
reflect the antiquity of the garments.
Frockmevintagefashion.com

HORNETS

Long-established in Kensington, this trio of shops is bursting with quality gentlemen's jackets, suits, hats (new and second-hand), shoes, ties and cravats.
Hornetskensington.co.uk
36b Kensington Church Street, London, W8 4BX
020 7937 262

LUCAS T LUCAS

A delightful and eccentric vintage clothing emporium at the ends of the earth, run by the genial Lucas, who also sells stuffed birds, antlers and ancient radiograms.
51 Market Jew Street, Penzance, Cornwall, TR18 2HZ
01734 364 280

OLD HAT

Vintage raiment for the discerning gent, specialising in second-hand bespoke suits for town and country.
66 Fulham High Street, London, SW6 3LQ
020 7610 6558

THE REAL McCOY

A musty cavern in the heart of Devonshire with very fairly priced vintage wear for ladies and gentlemen.
Therealmccoy.co.uk
21 McCoys Arcade, Fore Street, Exeter, Devon, England, EX4 3AN
01392 410481

SABRE SALES

A wide variety of genuine military wear for sale and hire, including webbing, uniforms, caps, boots, cloth insignia, buttons, divisional patches and air raid sirens.
Sabresales.co.uk
85-87 Castle Road, Southsea, Hampshire, PO5 3AY
02392 833394.

SAVVY ROW

An extremely convenient on-line service with home delivery and new stock arriving daily. Savvy Row also specialises in sourcing rare vintage for serious collectors.
Savvyrow.co.uk
6 Ivesley Cottages, Waterhouses, County Durham, DH7 9AY
0191 3737664

THE SOUK

A treasure trove in the heart of Bronte country with a plethora of heavy vintage tweeds for stalking across the moors.
The-souk.com
117 Main Street, Haworth, West Yorkshire, BD22 8DP
01535 646538

VINTAGE TO VOGUE

A rather stylish looking enterprise featuring men and women's vintage clothing and a selection of accessories, including jewellery.
Vintagetovoguebath.com
28 Milsom Street, Bath, BA1 1DG
01225 337323

VINTAGE WHISTLES

The gentleman's clothing and accessories range is extensive and Harris Tweed jackets are to be found in abundance, along with all the ephemera one would need for the lifestyle of a Bright Young Thing.
Vintagewhistles.co.uk
01733 706353

FOGEY UNLIMITED

Gentlemen's vintage clothing and brand-new dead stock from the past, some in its original packaging. If your underpants are not sufficiently retro, this is the place for you.
Fogeyunlimited.co.uk

FOOTWEAR

The following are all reputable makers of Goodyear-welted shoes and boots for gentlemen. Additional branches are listed on their web sites.

CHEANEY SHOES

Cheaney.co.uk
Rushton Road, Desborough, Kettering, Northamptonshire, NN14 2RZ
01536 760383

CHURCH & CO

Church-footwear.com
133 New Bond Street, Mayfair, London, W1S 2TE
0207 493 1474

CROCKETT & JONES
Crockettandjones.co.uk
69 Jermyn Street, London, SW1Y 6PF
0207 9672684

TRICKERS
Trickers.com
67 Jermyn Street, St. James's, London, SW1
01604 630595

HERRING SHOES
On-line vendors of quality footwear,
some made by Loake and others from
well-known brands such as Church and
Cheaney.
Herringshoes.co.uk
Old Station Yard, Kingsbridge, Devon,
TQ7 1ES
01548 854886

JEFFREY-WEST
For the more contemporary-minded
fellow, the shoes are nevertheless
Northampton-produced and of excellent
quality.
Jeffery-west.co.uk
Head Office: City House, 43 Cliftonville
Rd., Northampton, NN1 5HQ
01604 602 075

LOAKE
Avoid the cheaper end of their catalogue
and you will be shod in perfectly well-
made footwear.
Loake.co.uk
Loake Bros Ltd. Wood Street Kettering,
Northamptonshire, NN16 9SN
01536315900

WILLIAM LENNON & CO
On-line purveyor of replica Great War
army boots, but expect to wait almost as
long as the war for them to make them.
Williamlennon.co.uk
Stoney Middleton, Hope Valley, Derbyshire,
S32 4TD
01433 630 451

SHOE REPAIR

FIFTH AVENUE SHOE REPAIR
It is difficult to find someone you can
trust with your age-old trusty brogues, but
this little shop run by an Italian family can
handle a proper shoe, and also sells a good
range of new footwear.
Fifthavenueshoerepairs.com
41 Goodge Street, London, W1T 2PY
020 7636 6705

BRACES/SOCK SUSPENDERS

ALBERT THURSTON
Albert Thurston began making braces and
sock suspenders in 1820, and is still the
last word in trouser and hosiery support.
Albertthurston.com

THE CHAP SHOP
On-line retailer of gentlemen's accessories,
including braces with flat ends for that
1940s high-waisted trouser look.
www.thechap.net

CUFFLINKS

CHARLES TYRWHITT
A decent range of affordable cufflinks to
go with their similarly fulsome range of
French-cuffed shirts.
Ctshirts.co.uk
92 Jermyn Street, London, SW1Y 6JB
020 7839 6060

LONGMIRE
The Longmire Rose Gold collection is
possibly the finest on offer, with hand
carved cufflinks in 18k gold, hand set gems
and mother of pearl ovals.
Longmire.co.uk
12 Bury Street, St James's, London, SW1
10 New Bond Street, London, W1
020 7930 8720

T. M. LEWIN
In-house designed cufflinks to compliment
their range of shirts, including colourific
enamels, bold features and, God forbid, a
range of "humorous" designs.
Tmlewin.co.uk
103-108 Jermyn Street, London, SW1Y
6EQ
020 7839 3372

EYEWEAR

DEAD MEN'S SPEX
Genuine vintage glasses and retro
spectacles ranging from the 1850s to the
1970s.
Deadmensspex.com
4 Gunn St, Foulsham, Norfolk, NR20 5RJ
0797 177 8095

OPERA OPERA
Operaopera.net
98 Long Acre, Covent Garden, London,
WC2E 9NR
020 7836 9246

RETROSPECS
Many of the vast selection of frames are genuine vintage, while others are well-crafted reproductions. All frames can be fitted with ophthalmic lenses.
Retrospecs.co.uk
Robert Roope Opticians, 20 George St, St Albans, Hertfordshire, AL3 4ES
01727 761048

SPECSAVERS
Don't be alarmed; they only get a mention for re-introducing the monocle - a commendable contribution to gentlemanly optics.
Specsavers.co.uk

GLOVES

BLACK
Specialist in men's driving gloves, including chamois deerskins or cotton and tobacco deerskin with classic wrist strap.
Black.co.uk
01342 715505

SERMONETA
An Italian family-owned artisan workshop with a shop on Burlington Arcade redolent of a Regency store.
Sermonetagloves.com
51 Burlington Arcade, London, W1J 0QJ
020 7491 9009

MR SWANTONS
Masters of the tonsorial art of barbering, one can sit back and relax confidently in traditional decor without fear of female intrusion, since Mr Swanton famously bans women from entering the premises.
3, Bruton Place, Bristol, Avon BS8 1JN
0117 973 6157

TRUMPERS
The original Curzon Street shop has a stunning decor of mahogany-panelled private cubicles. Services supplied are haircutting, tinting, moustache and beard trimming, shaving, manicure, pedicure, facial cleanse and massage.
Trumpers.com
9 Curzon Street, London, W1J 5HQ
020 7499 1850

TAYLOR OF OLD BOND STREET
Not just a splendid St James's shop, but also a wealth of grooming products available on-line as well, including moustache wax.
74 Jermyn Street, St James's, London, SW1Y 6NP
020 7930 5544/5321

MR. WAX
The eponymous Mr. Wax was so fed up with ineffectual moustache wax that he created his own brand, Bounder "tested on gentlemen, not animals".
www.mr-wax.com

GROOMING

CARTER AND BOND
Originally an online purveyor of traditional grooming products including open razors, double-edged safety razors, shaving brushes, traditional shaving preparations, moustache waxes, hair pomades, now also a gentlemens barbershop.
carterandbond.com
83 Westbourne Park Road
London
W2 5QH
020 7727 3141

LUGGAGE

GLOBE TROTTER
Strong yet lightweight functionality with an instantly recognisable vintage design aesthetic.
Globe-trotterltd.com
54-55 Burlington Arcade, Mayfair, London W1J 0LB
020 7529 5950

ORIGINAL VINTAGE LUGGAGE
If you're wondering where to snag a classic piece of antique luggage, try this superb collection of original vintage items, sourced as far back at the 1800s
Originalvintageluggage.com
Unit D37, Stables Market, Camden Lock, NW10, London W10

MENDING/RESTORATION

BRITISH INVISIBLE MENDING SERVICE LTD
Repairs damage to cloth by extracting individual threads from a concealed part of the garment and weaving them over the damaged area, making holes and tears completely disappear.
Invisiblemending.co.uk
32 Thayer Street, London, W1U 2QT
Head Office: 0144343334
Retail: 0207 4874292

ROSARIO TAILORING
A fresh and modern approach to the tailoring business, offering high quality work on restyling, remodelling and altering hemlines and waistlines.
Rosariotailoring.co.uk
Unit 10 Archer Street Studios, 10-11 Archer Street, London, W1D 7AZ
020 72870458

UMBRELLA/ WALKING CANE SUPPLIERS

FOX UMBRELLAS
A factory in Surrey with an on-line emporium of quality gentlemen's umbrellas.
Foxumbrellas.co.uk
240a Wickham Road, Shirley, Croydon, Surrey, CR0 8BJ
020 8662 0022

T.FOX & CO
Not to be confused with the above, this is a discreet little umbrella shop in the City with a listed shop sign that cannot be changed.
Tfox.co.uk
118 London Wall, London, EC2Y 5JA
0207 628 1868

GEOFFREY BREEZE ANTIQUE CANES
Purveyor of a vast selection of antique gentlemen's canes, swagger sticks and umbrellas dating back to the 18th century.
Antiquecanes.co.uk
Office 262, 3 Edgar Buildings, George Street, Bath, BA1 2FJ
077 404 35844

JAMES SMITH & SONS
Rather unfriendly but still worth a visit for the delightful Victorian shop front alone and the wealth of canes and umbrellas.
James-smith.co.uk
53 New Oxford Street, London, WC1A 1BL
0207 836 4731

WATCHES

CORR VINTAGE WATCHES
Classic vintage Swiss watches from dress to military in outstanding condition.
www.corrvintagewatches.com
020 7923 7687

OGDEN OF HARROGATE
New and vintage gentlemen's timepieces in a shop dating back to 1893. J.R. Ogden accompanied Howard Carter at the opening of the Tomb of Tutankhamun in 1922.
Ogdenharrogate.co.uk
38 James Street, Harrogate, North Yorkshire, UK, HG1 1RQ
01423 504123

PIECES OF TIME
Claims to be the largest catalogue of pocket watches and movements in the world.
Antique-watch.com
1-7 Davies Mews, London, W1Y 2LP
0207 629 2422

WATCH ME GO
An online trove of vintage and designer watches of every period and description, with free UK delivery.
Watchmego.co.uk
79 Grosvenor Avenue, London, N5 2NN
020 7503 5454

FURTHER READING

If you have enjoyed reading this book, you might like to continue in the same vein by reading The Chap, a magazine for the modern gentleman. It features a regular "Am I A Chap?" section, as well as features, stories and articles about how to live your life with a dash of flair and panache, while retaining your sense of humour and without necessarily being fabulously wealthy.
Subscribe or buy individual issues on-line at www.thechap.net